Praise for *Flexible Leadership*

"Kevin has a long history of understanding developing challenges in the world of business leadership and bringing timely insight to the everyday leader. Once again he does not disappoint. *Flexible Leadership* is an excellent guide to modern situational leadership in an increasingly connected and complex work environment. Most importantly, this work provides profound insight on how to put these critical new principles to work in your personal leadership journey today."

—Kent Womack, Senior Vice President, Operations, American Soda LLC

"Kevin Eikenberry has been a mentor and thought partner in my leadership journey for nearly two decades. His latest book, *Flexible Leadership*, distills the mindset, skillset, and habits needed to thrive in today's complex environment. Kevin's real-world insights make this book a practical playbook for leaders at any stage. His authentic and flexible approach has shaped my own leadership philosophy, and I know it will resonate deeply with others seeking to lead with clarity and confidence."

—Scott Blecke, CEO, Yampa Valley Electric Association

"In a time when authentic leadership is more crucial than ever, *Flexible Leadership* offers a timely and refreshing approach. Grounded in the study of opposites, it provides a rooted foundation from which confident, balanced decisions can grow. From this solid base comes the development and growth every leader seeks, with pragmatic, flexible strategies that are truly applicable to day-in, day-out leadership moments. It's an essential guide for those ready to lead with clarity, adaptability, and purpose."

—Scott Allison, Vice President, Professional Services, MyEyeDr.

"In a world where leadership has become increasingly complex, *Flexible Leadership* emerges as a timely and essential guide. Drawing on years of experience and a deep understanding of today's leadership challenges, Kevin offers a clear path forward for anyone committed to leading effectively in uncertain times. This book goes beyond mere advice; it's a comprehensive tool kit designed to equip leaders with the flexibility and adaptability necessary to thrive in today's fast-paced environment.

What makes *Flexible Leadership* truly stand out is its focus on actionable insights that are both profound and practical. Kevin masterfully distills the core of flexible leadership, offering strategies that apply directly to real-world situations, making the content accessible to leaders at every level. The book speaks to the heart of what it means to lead with confidence—without relying on rigid frameworks—and offers a refreshing approach to navigating change while maintaining clarity and purpose.

As you read, you'll discover how to embrace flexibility, not just as an option but as a core leadership strength. Kevin challenges outdated notions, inspiring leaders to evolve by providing both the mindset and tools necessary to create lasting impact. This book is an invitation to rethink leadership and to build a legacy that adapts to the complexities of our time. If you're looking for a road map to elevate your leadership journey, *Flexible Leadership* is exactly the guide you need."

—Kavita Kurup, Global Head, Human Resources, UST

"No matter how experienced you may be as a leader, *Flexible Leadership* will give you new ways to think about how you lead every day. Kevin provides a great framework to help readers consider what type of leadership is needed in different situations instead of falling back on their preferred leadership style. This book is one worth revisiting often to keep your leadership in balance."

—Christy Denault, Vice President, Marketing and
Communications, National Precast Concrete Association

FLEXIBLE
LEADERSHIP

Also by Kevin Eikenberry

Vantagepoints on Learning and Life

*Remarkable Leadership: Unleashing Your
Leadership Potential One Skill at a Time*

*#Leadershiptweet Book01: 140 Bite-Sized Ideas to Help
You Become the Leader You Were Born to Be*

*Remarkable Leadership Facilitator's Guide: Twelve
Programs for Creating Remarkable Leaders*

*From Bud to Boss: Secrets to a Successful Transition
to Remarkable Leadership* (with Guy Harris)

My Journey from Bud to Boss (with Guy Harris and Sara Jane Hope)

*The Long-Distance Leader: Rules for Remarkable
Remote Leadership* (with Wayne Turmel)

*The Long-Distance Teammate: Stay Engaged and Connected
While Working Anywhere* (with Wayne Turmel)

*The Long-Distance Team: Designing Your Team for
Everyone's Success* (with Wayne Turmel)

*The Long-Distance Leader, Second Edition: Revised Rules for
Remarkable Remote and Hybrid Leadership* (with Wayne Turmel)

FLEXIBLE LEADERSHIP

Navigate Uncertainty and Lead with Confidence

KEVIN EIKENBERRY

Matt Holt Books
An Imprint of BenBella Books, Inc.
Dallas, TX

Matt Holt is an imprint of BenBella Books, Inc.
8080 N. Central Expressway
Suite 1700
Dallas, TX 75206
benbellabooks.com
Send feedback to feedback@benbellabooks.com

BenBella and *Matt Holt* are federally registered trademarks.

Printed in the United States of America
10 9 8 7 6 5 4 3 2 1

Library of Congress Control Number: 2024038101
ISBN 9781637746318 (hardcover)
ISBN 9781637746325 (electronic)

Editing by Lydia Choi
Copyediting by Michael Fedison
Proofreading by Jenny Bridges and Ashley Casteel
Text design and composition by PerfecType, Nashville, TN
Cover design by Morgan Carr
Printed by Lake Book Manufacturing

Special discounts for bulk sales are available. Please contact bulkorders@benbellabooks.com.

To all those who have helped me become a more effective and confident (Remarkable and Flexible!) leader—including those I have read and listened to, lived with, loved, led, been led by, observed, and coached.

All of you have given me the chance to learn, grow, and improve. This book is for you.

CONTENTS

SECTION 3: THE HABITSET OF FLEXIBLE LEADERS | 155

FOREWORD

In this era of unprecedented change and challenge, the leadership landscape is rapidly evolving, demanding a fresh approach and new capabilities from those who've dedicated themselves to leading others.

Flexible Leadership: Navigate Uncertainty and Lead with Confidence by Kevin Eikenberry has arrived at the perfect moment. This book is not just timely; *it is essential.* And like a lighthouse on the shoreline, it offers a beacon for those navigating these turbulent times, especially for those attempting to guide teams and organizations.

Full disclosure: I've known Kevin Eikenberry for many years. I've been an avid reader of his books and a devoted listener of his teachings. In my view, he stands out as a true visionary in the field of leadership. Kevin's deep expertise and compassionate approach have already transformed countless leadership journeys, including mine.

In Kevin's newest book, he shares even deeper insights that are both profound and practical, drawn from a career dedicated to understanding and enhancing how leaders succeed.

What makes this book a pivotal read is its core message: *the power of flexibility in leadership.* Kevin expertly makes the case for flexibility, not as a nice-to-have but as an essential trait for today's leaders. He guides us away from outdated, rigid models toward a dynamic, responsive leadership style that will enable every leader who reads and applies it to thrive even in times of complexity and change.

The genius of Kevin's writing lies in how it equips us with the mindset, skillset, and habitset necessary to lead effectively, no matter the circumstances. But what connects most deeply with me is that his strategies are grounded in real-world application, making them accessible to leaders at all levels—from those just starting out to seasoned executives.

As you turn these pages, you'll find yourself immersed in a master class in leadership. Kevin's engaging narrative is not only instructive but also incredibly inspiring. His words encourage us to challenge our preconceptions, embrace adaptability, and lead with renewed confidence and clarity.

Four key elements stand out to me in this powerful book, and I offer them not as a summary, but instead as an exciting preview of what's ahead for you as a reader:

1. **Evolution of Leadership**: Kevin emphasizes the continuous evolution of our leadership approach as necessary to meet modern challenges. If you're holding tight to outdated methods and ideas, prepare to have your perspective expanded.

2. **The Power of Flexibility**: He champions flexibility as a critical leadership attribute, pushing us to blend consistency with adaptability for optimal results. Flexibility is not "soft"—it's a solid leadership attribute that enables a leader to navigate accountability and engagement in a way that creates true commitment.

3. **Practical Wisdom**: This is not a book that seeks to impress with abstract ideas, sophisticated theories, or complex systems. Instead, this book is filled with actionable insights, each of which is deeply rooted in Kevin's extensive experience and his empathetic understanding of the leadership journey.

4. **Empowering and Inspirational**: You may buy this book to learn new ideas, but you'll finish it feeling inspired. Kevin's supportive voice and profound insights empower you to transform your approach to leadership and leave you passionately dedicated to becoming a better leader.

In writing this foreword, I am not just introducing a book; I am inviting you to experience a transformative leadership philosophy—one that will not only drive extraordinary results but can also shape your leadership legacy.

Kevin Eikenberry's *Flexible Leadership* is more than a guide—*it is a mentor in print*, ready to help you navigate the complexities of leadership with grace and effectiveness.

Jim Huling

Executive coach and coauthor of *The 4 Disciplines of Execution*

INTRODUCTION

Here's Where We Are

Leadership is complicated and difficult. That's always been true but is truer now than ever. If you long for a return to the "good old days" of less complications and more certainty, it is time to wake up. The context in which we lead and work in the future will be trickier and more entangled. And yet, in the most important ways, the essence and goals of leadership haven't changed, nor do I believe they ever will.

Everything seems to be changing, yet the most important things *aren't changing at all*.

This is the first of many paradoxes you will be reminded of or discover in this book.

In a world that is growing more complicated, complex, and challenging, we must find ways to understand that context without losing sight of what matters most. That is the big idea and big goal of this book: to help us see the complexity, embrace it, and operate within it without losing our heads or creating confusion for ourselves and our teams.

Getting this right is a big deal for everyone.

Organizationally, we've been trying to get leadership development right for far longer than I've been in the working world (call that 1985). Smart people have built approaches and models and assessments to help us. And smart, well-meaning organizations have invested in using and providing training on those models and tools. Why? Because both the research and personal experience tell us that the companies that get the best results have more effective leaders.

And the results of these efforts and the return on many of these investments has ranged from abysmal to greatly disappointing. Research from McKinsey & Company found that only 11% of executives believe their leadership development activities "achieve and sustain the desired results."[1] But because having more effective leaders is important, we keep investing, and keep hoping, and while some people improve, organizationally we keep being disappointed.

It's understandable, but it isn't hard to see that this is an (expensive) example of Einstein's definition of insanity: doing the same things and expecting a new result. If you picked up this book wanting to more effectively develop leaders across your organization, you are in the right place (and make sure you read the final chapter—it is just for you).

At least some individual leaders want to improve too. They want their work to be easier, perhaps, but more likely they see leadership as a way to make a positive difference for their organizations and their teams. It is a worthy goal to make a positive impact and improve their career trajectory by being a more effective leader. There are plenty of reasons why they eagerly take the training that is offered. They read books and hire coaches to figure out how to be more effective at this challenging work. Since you are reading these words, it is likely you are one of those leaders.

That's why, from now on, the "they" is you. I am writing for and to you (and me) as leaders striving to grow and improve our results and impact.

And as much as organizations want to develop leaders, and many individual leaders want to crack the code and become more effective, our team members are begging for us all to figure it out too. People want to work where they have a boss they know, like, and trust. They yearn for a role where they are clear on what is expected of them, feel like they can grow, and know they are making a difference. The chances for those things to happen without a strong leader aren't very good.

The cynic would say that another book isn't going to solve all these problems and relieve all the frustrations. Someone—likely you—with a more positive view says we need to solve them and expects this book to help.

If we are willing to change, the ideas in this book can make a difference and help us break the insanity cycle. We must be open to changing the way we see things so that we can solve the challenges we face in new ways. You've said this before: "Thinking about things the same way won't give us new ideas or solutions."

You were right when you said that—and it is that same approach, looking at the situation differently, that gives us a shot at transformational improvement.

It won't be easy—and it can't be—because I am challenging you to rethink your foundational thoughts about yourself and what it means to lead effectively. I will urge you to look at the world as it is—not as we have seen it before or wish it to be. Through all of that, I am going to give you hope.

Because the path of Flexible Leadership can help any leader get better results with greater frequency while building confidence, hope, and assurance—even in a world full of uncertainty.

If that sounds like something that matters to you and your organization, you are in the right place.

Let's go.

THE MINDSET OF FLEXIBLE LEADERS

Most of what is written to help leaders become more effective focuses on the skills they need. Yet skills alone aren't enough. To become a better, more remarkable, more confident, and, yes, a more flexible leader requires more than skills.

Your success is most possible when you align your *mindset* with the necessary *skillset* and translate it into a new *habitset*.

The book is broken into sections on each of these:

- Section 1: The Mindset of Flexible Leaders
- Section 2: The Skillset of Flexible Leaders
- Section 3: The Habitset of Flexible Leaders

You may be tempted to skip to section 2, where you will find the "how-tos" of Flexible Leadership. It is your book, and of course you can read it and use it however you wish. But since my hope is for this book to be a positive turning point in your career, success, satisfaction, and impact, I urge you to read section 1 first. With the right background and perspectives, the skills will make more sense and be far easier to implement.

CHAPTER 1

STARTING AT THE BEGINNING

Everything begins at the beginning, and quite often the beginning begins when you shift your mind in a new direction.

—Louie Herron, entrepreneur, coach, and author[2]

Julie Andrews told us in *The Sound of Music* that starting at the beginning is a very good place to start.

And I agree.

The starting point for our journey together is the title of the book.

Flexible Leadership: Navigate Uncertainty and Lead with Confidence

We are going to start by getting greater clarity on the familiar words in this title, because once we have that, we will be better prepared for the success we desire.

Let's look at each of the key words in the title.

FLEXIBLE

Flexible might not be a word at the top of your list of leadership attributes . . . yet. But by the time you finish this book and apply the ideas you'll gain, I believe it will be at or near the top of your list. What does it mean to be flexible?

According to Merriam-Webster,[3] here are the definitions of the word *flexible*:

1. Capable of being flexed: Pliant (for example, flexible branches swaying in the breeze)
2. Yielding to influence: Tractable (for example, a flexible person without strong convictions)
3. Characterized by a ready capability to adapt to new, different, or changing requirements (for example, a flexible foreign policy or a flexible schedule)

Do you want a leader with these qualities? And do you want those qualities for yourself? For me, the answer is yes for all three. Here's why:

1. While the branch is pliant, the tree is rooted firmly. A leader who is "capable of being flexed" yet is still rooted by ethics, principles, and values is the leader others will follow.
2. While I don't care for the example including "without strong convictions," I love the idea of a leader being willing to be influenced. Don't we want leaders who will listen to the input of their teams and be flexible in the face of new or divergent information?
3. Chances are you feel that the world and the requirements placed on you are changing. If so, you know you need to adapt—which is the third definition of *flexible*.

To further our initial understanding of the word, here are some synonyms for *flexible*: adaptable, changeable, malleable, variable, adjustable, elastic, modifiable, fluid, pliable. All these words are instructive as we think about how we lead and are perceived by others.

Take a few minutes to consider how you feel about these words and the concept of being more flexible. How much do you think you adapt, modify, and flex your approaches currently? How would you predict your team might answer that question?

FLEXIBLE LEADERSHIP

Maybe this idea of Flexible Leadership is a pretty good idea.

But part of you is thinking, *Wait, wait, wait! Don't we want leaders to be consistent? Aren't we losing consistency if we strive for flexibility?*

Consistency in some things is desired, for sure. Here are some important examples:

- *Consistency builds trust.* When we are consistent in our words and actions, people know what to expect from us.
- *Consistency builds credibility.* When we are consistent in our ethical standards, we enhance our credibility.
- *Consistency supports equity and fairness.* When rules and standards are applied consistently, there will likely be less division and more team cohesion.
- *Consistency supports stability.* When leaders are consistent in times of stress or uncertainty, they help the team feel more secure.

All of these are true.

And . . .

Flexible Leadership isn't at odds with consistency. Because we don't need to frame flexibility and consistency as opposites. If they were opposites, then the antonyms of our flexibility definitions would be instructive. Let's look at some of those antonyms.

- Established
- Stable
- Fixed
- Rigid
- Strict
- Hard
- Severe
- Harsh
- Stiff

While the first two seem useful, what about the rest?

Do you want to be a leader (or to be led by someone) who is seen as rigid, strict, hard, severe, stiff, or harsh?

Not so much. (Neither does your team.)

If you don't frame consistency and flexibility as opposites, how do you think about them?

You frame them as both valuable *and* helpful, even though they aren't the same. When you do that, *you move from either/or thinking to both/and thinking.*

One of the problems I just uncovered, which is a major point of this book, is that it is easier and more common to label ourselves as just one thing—to think either/or.

- A consistent leader
- A facilitative leader

- A servant leader
- A [name your style based on the assessment you took] leader

When we label ourselves as one type of leader (because we have been told to or because we took an assessment) or consider a situation from only one perspective or lens, we begin to look for the "right" answer. There must be a right answer—right?

What if we looked for *best* answers, rather than right ones?

Being a Flexible Leader means you can be consistent, facilitative, in service to others, and 20 other things, *whenever that particular trait or behavior is most needed or helpful.*

This means that being flexible is harder because it urges us to look for *best* (or even possible) answers for the situation, not *right* answers. Nor does it mean we should simply lean into "who we are." It requires us to think, to take in the context, to consider the individuals involved, and to look at the situation holistically.

If you only prioritize consistency and choose to act based on your habits, experience, style, or strengths, you may (and many do) say, "This is my style—here I am; take it or leave it," or, "I'm going to do it this way because that's who I am." That's a clear, understandable, and *easier* approach than choosing to be flexible.

Clear, understandable, and easier—but not necessarily more effective.

Because leadership isn't about us.

In the book *The Long-Distance Leader: Rules for Remarkable Remote Leadership* (which I coauthored with Wayne Turmel), we introduced the 3O Model of Leadership.

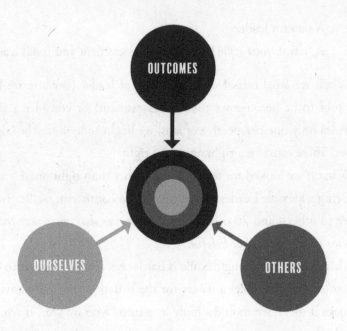

It visually represents what leadership is: reaching valuable outcomes with and through others. Outcomes matter, and so do the people doing the work. And both of those factors take precedence over us as the leader. Putting ourselves in the middle doesn't make leadership about us but reminds us that who we are and how we lead has a huge impact on the other two: outcomes and others. I propose that when we define ourselves not as we have seen ourselves in the past or by our style but instead as a Flexible Leader, we will be far more effective at reaching valuable outcomes with and through others.

When we lead in flexible ways, we can serve outcomes and others in big ways. We can still connect to our mission, our purpose, and our values. And we can flex and be authentic and genuine and, yes, even transparent.

Being a Flexible Leader doesn't mean flip-flopping or that people won't have any sense of where you're coming from. When a Flexible Leader is purposeful and prioritizes based on purpose, people will recognize and appreciate it. If you want to be the leader you were born to be and that your organization and team want and need you to be, are you ready, willing, and able to adapt to new, different, or changing requirements? (There's the third definition of *flexible*.)

Hopefully this all sounds good. But before we move on, recognize that the journey of being a Flexible Leader is a harder choice. It will require you to move past your habits, your comfort zone, how you view yourself as a leader. It might even challenge some of what you have learned about leadership.

But the effort is worth it. It will help you develop and nurture individuals and a team that will achieve amazing outcomes. And it will transform your personal success and confidence at the same time. You may not believe me yet, but you will.

NAVIGATE

The next key word in the title is *navigate*. The root word in *navigate* is *navigare*, which hints at sailing and steering a ship. As leaders, we are steering a ship toward our desired destination or outcome. I am not a sailor or a boater, so my thinking here is metaphorical, not personal. But I know that when I am on a boat, I want the captain to be steering based on knowing where we are and where we are going. To navigate anything, whether a cash flow crisis, a new product launch, a reorg, or just daily work, requires a good sense of where we are and where we are going.

To navigate requires skills, for sure, but it also requires awareness of the situation and your location. Leaders don't simply exist, and they do more than steer—they move on the waves of time and change, doing whatever is needed to reach a destination. To navigate implies subtlety and skill. The next chapter will provide us with a more helpful and accurate map to help us navigate the uncertainties we encounter with far greater confidence.

UNCERTAINTY

For 70 years, researchers have known that people don't love uncertainty. Imagine if you had been a part of Daniel Ellsberg's famous experiments, beginning in 1961. Here is the situation. You walk into a room with two urns filled with colored balls. You're told one urn has 100 balls, 50 white and 50 black. The other urn also has 100 black and white balls in it, but you aren't told the number of each color. You are told one ball will be picked from one of the urns, and you must bet $100 on which color it will be. Then you get to pick which urn.

Which urn would you pick from?

If you chose the urn with 50 black and 50 white balls, welcome to the club—that is the urn most people would pick from.

It isn't math or logic that leads to that conclusion, but Ellsberg repeatedly found that is what most people pick. It's called the Ellsberg paradox: people will steer away from the uncertain option. (By the way, his findings have been repeatedly tested in a variety of ways since his initial work, all with the same result.)

The research proves what you already know—uncertainty isn't our favorite thing. Here are just some of the problems it can cause for us:

- *Increases in anxiety and stress.* When we can't predict outcomes or understand what the future holds, our body's stress response can be triggered.
- *Decision-making difficulty.* When outcomes are uncertain, we often avoid decisions or become paralyzed by them.

- *Mental health challenges.* Long exposure to uncertainty can lead to deep anxiety or depression.
- *Reduced sense of control.* When things are uncertain and we feel we can't impact outcomes, motivation can drop, and our feelings of helplessness can grow.
- *Increased cognitive load and fatigue.* When we feel too much uncertainty, we can experience decision fatigue and a reduced ability to complete other tasks. This can hurt our judgment and focus and limit our ability to solve problems.
- *Relationship challenges.* Uncertainty can strain relationships (including at work) due to reduced or ineffective communication practices and perhaps increased conflict within those relationships.

When we think about how much uncertainty we face at work and then look at these challenges, it is easy to see how uncertainty is perhaps an under-recognized problem in the workplace today. For us to lead effectively, we must learn how to navigate it more effectively and help our teams do the same.

Which is worse: Uncertainty or fear?

The research on this question is clear—and might be surprising to you.

One of the ways our response to uncertainty has been researched is through using electric shocks. Let's imagine ourselves in another study (this one from 1992). You are placed in one of two groups, and everyone in both groups is informed that they will receive 20 electric shocks, either moderate or strong. (Aren't you glad we are only imagining this?)

One group receives 20 strong shocks.

The other group receives 17 strong shocks, with 3 moderate shocks randomly interspersed between them.

Which group would you rather be in?

You might like the idea of some moderate shocks. But that group—those who didn't know how strong the next shock would be—experienced significantly more stress than the other.

More recent research shows (still using electric shocks) that stress increases not based on the level of pain but on the amount of uncertainty that we feel. As my friend Ashley Goodall says in his book *The Problem with Change*, "the implication of this finding is that no news, for us humans, is actually worse than bad news, particularly when it's not clear which way events are going to go."[4]

There is a difference between fear and anxiety. Fear comes with an ending. Psychologist Martin Seligman encourages us to think about fear like a rabid dog. If the dog is nearby, we are fearful of being bitten. If we are told the dog has been removed from the area (and we know that), the fear dissipates. But we would remain anxious if we didn't know where the dog went—similarly, anxiety is less specific than fear and, according to Seligman, "more chronic and not bound to an object." If there isn't a specific thing to connect our feelings to—in other words, if we can't remove it—the anxiety remains.

Uncertainty, then, is worse than fear—because we can't see the end to it.

I'm guessing you have examples of that in your work and life. Several probably come to mind immediately.

While we can't remove all uncertainty from our world, we can frame it differently, allowing us to navigate it more effectively. And the tools to do that are in this book.

CONFIDENCE

Confidence is something we all want and that we know is valuable. Simply stated, it is an expectation of success. It is a sense that we can deal with the uncertainty, and we will do fine (or better).

How important is confidence at work?

I could share research to answer this question, but instead let's do some personal reflection. Think about a time in your life (at work or otherwise) when you had a healthy level of confidence. Once you have your example in mind, think about the results you achieved after the event or situation.

- How was your stress level?
- What did your results look like?
- And how much of a role did your confidence have in those results?

I bet I know the short answers to these questions:

- Manageable or low
- Good or excellent
- Quite a bit

When we don't feel confident about a situation, we generally approach it with timidity, caution, and perhaps anxiety. We wonder and worry about what will happen and how we will perform. (There's that uncertainty again.)

Think about it: How many of those things—timidity, caution, and anxiety—will help you be more effective?

But when we are confident, we experience the opposite of many of the things just mentioned. First, you become more willing to try something (which is important if there is something at work you really need to do). Beyond that, you gain greater mental fitness, meaning you will have:

- *Less stress.* While some amount of stress can be helpful, generally when you feel less stress you are better able to perform.
- *Less fear.* The fear may be of failure, of looking bad, or of any other scary consequences. Fear tends to immobilize us and keeps us from operating and thinking clearly and effectively.
- *Less performance anxiety.* When we are confident, not only do we have the courage to begin, but we also are far more likely to be mentally present as we perform, which helps us perform even better.

Ultimately, beyond the mental benefits we gain from greater confidence at work, both before and during the work, we will get better results, higher-quality results, more consistent results—and in doing so, we trigger the confidence/competence loop.

The confidence/competence loop?

We all recognize that our success accelerates when we are confident. The reason is simple. Without confidence, we focus on uncertainty and fear. And when we are fearful, we don't take any action. We get tentative, we delay, and we procrastinate. When we let go of our fear, we act more quickly and easily.

Fine, but the practical question remains: How do I become more confident? The simplest answer is to become more competent. As we become more skilled at a task, our fear shrinks, and our confidence grows. This is the crux of the confidence/competence loop. And as our confidence grows, we get better (more competent). So these two critical factors for our success at anything (including any skill at work) are forever joined.

Here's an example.

Let's take a task you likely know how to do well—like riding a bicycle. Are you afraid to ride a bike? Likely not, because you know how to do it. If I give you a bicycle and invite you to ride, you likely will do it right away. There is no reason to delay, there is no real fear—you just ride.

However, the longer it has been since you have ridden, the more your confidence might drop (and fear might climb). And if I gave you a unicycle instead, you would be very uncertain, and your fear would likely grow—a lot. Like most people, you wouldn't even get on the seat.

I told myself once that I wanted to ride a unicycle. I even bought one. But the fear of falling and the uncertainty of what a broken leg (or worse) would do to my fledgling business kept both my feet on the ground and eventually put the unicycle in the attic.

So how do we get started?

We put our butt in the seat. (Something I never *really* did with the unicycle.) And pedal.

Action overcomes fear. And with action, we have the starting point of competence. Because we can't get good at anything until we try it. There is a famous book from the 1980s called *Feel the Fear and Do It Anyway* by Susan Jeffers. It is a great title, but even better advice. If you want to start the confidence/competence loop, you simply have to start.

And . . .

Once you start doing things that used to scare you, your confidence will increase. And once you keep trying, you build skills. When you notice your skills improving, you get even more confident. More confidence in your skills makes it easier to improve them even more.

And so on, and so on.

While the research calls this a loop, I like to think of it as an upward spiral with both confidence and competence growing each time.

Confidence, competence, confidence, competence.

This loop is incredibly important for us individually, especially in building our confidence and competence at the complex skillset for leading others.

But this loop applies to the members of our team too. As you move through this book, you will see plenty of ways and times you can help your team and individual team members "spin" the confidence/competence loop.

However this book arrived in your hands or on your device, I hope now you are both clearer about the opportunity in front of you and more excited about becoming a Flexible Leader.

PAUSE AND REFLECT

Before you move on, take a minute to think about these questions. (Even better if you take some notes on your thoughts!)

- How do I feel about the idea of being more flexible? Does that word create hope, trepidation, or both?
- What are the uncertainties I am thinking about right now?
- What is my level of confidence as a leader?
- Which of the ideas in this chapter excites me most as I move to the next chapter?

RESOURCES TO HELP YOU LEAD FLEXIBLY

If you want to dive deeper into building confidence in yourself and others, we offer a Remarkable Master Class that will help. You can learn more at RemarkableMasterClass.com or by scanning this QR code.

> This means that being flexible is harder because it urges us to look for *best* (or even possible) answers for the situation, not *right* answers. Nor does it mean we should simply lean into "who we are." It requires us to think, to take in the context, to consider the individuals involved, and to look at the situation holistically.

CHAPTER 2

SENSEMAKING FOR OUR SUCCESS

> An algorithm can arrive at optimization, but only a
> human being—an artist, a thinker, a mathematician, an
> entrepreneur, a politician—only someone with a sense of
> perspective can interpret the meaning of the destination.
> Masters spend their entire lives in pursuit of this interpre-
> tation. This is how they make sense of the world.
> —Christian Madsbjerg, author[5]

Imagine being dropped in an area remote to you, without a map or cell service, and knowing you needed to get to civilization. It isn't some new reality show, and it isn't a dream. It is a thought exercise. How would you feel in this situation?

Confused?

Concerned?

Worried?

Scared?

Immobilized?

Lost?

Back to reality. How often do you feel those same feelings as a leader in real life? Even the most confident and experienced among us are nodding our heads.

In our fictional frightful situation, what we want is a map. Maps give us a sense of our current location, the terrain around us, and the path or paths available to us. Maps help us navigate the world around us so we can reach our desired destination. With a map, we are less uncertain and feel like things will be better.

Even if you didn't realize it until now, as leaders we need maps too—a way to give us context and make sense of our situations. Because once we have that, while we may still feel worried, the other emotions may ease enough for us to feel less uncertain and be able to move forward.

As leaders, though, while we have phones with cell service and GPS, the worlds we are navigating don't show up on those screens. And even if they did, I would propose they are out of date (more on that later).

SENSEMAKING

Karl Weick, who introduced this word, defines it as "the ongoing retrospective development of plausible images that rationalize what people are doing."[6] Weick and other social psychologists use this phrase to help understand how groups make sense of things and reach decisions. I like an alternative definition, by Dave Snowden, whom you will meet soon. He says sensemaking is: *How do we make sense of the world so that we can act in it?* While both definitions are helpful, Snowden's is more personal and more directly connected to our conversation.

If you were in the remote place I mentally created for you, that is what you would want: some information to help you make sense of the world so you could act most effectively and appropriately. The context of the situation would be incredibly helpful.

Deborah Ancona, at the MIT Sloan School of Management, wrote in her paper "Sensemaking: Framing and Acting in the Unknown": "Sensemaking enables leaders to have a better grasp of what is going on in their environments, thus facilitating other leadership activities such as visioning, relating, and inventing."[7] But the benefits aren't just in those three areas. I propose that unless we have an accurate map of the world we work in, we can't consistently improve our ability to lead in any way at all.

THE CYNEFIN FRAMEWORK AND SENSEMAKING

Snowden developed and continues to refine a sensemaking model called the Cynefin Framework. *Cynefin* (ku-*nev*-in) is a Welsh word that is literally defined as "a habitat or place" but actually means the place of your multiple belongings—all of our experiences and "belongings" profoundly influence who we are (and how we lead), yet we can never fully grasp that complexity. It is a layered word that can help us understand the complex systems we lead in.

Since its creation in 1999 when Snowden worked for IBM Global Services, the Cynefin Framework has been used in many ways to look at and better understand complex systems. Most uses are for groups and organizations to understand big problems. It has been used to explore and better understand supply chain management, customer relations, policymaking, network science, emergency management, and more. It has been used as the basis for models of decision-making strategy. In fact, in 2007, Snowden and Mary E. Boone described the framework in an award-winning paper in the *Harvard Business Review* titled "A Leader's Framework for Decision Making."[8]

As you will see on page 27, this framework/map consists of four areas. Once we recognize we are on the map, we can begin to determine how to lead based on that context. If you were in the mountains, you would have some idea of what tools and gear you would need, which would be different from if you were on a secluded island or in a desert. The value of the Cynefin Framework is that it helps us identify our context more easily and clearly, because at work it isn't as obvious as seeing miles of sand, a forest, or mountains.

While the framework has been most often used in the big picture, in the *HBR* article, Snowden and Boone suggest a more personal use. Since then, Snowden has summarized that "Cynefin is fractal, it is self similar at multiple levels but can be understood simply or on further investigation in more complex ways."[9]

Being fractal means that it works in the big picture but in small situations too. This more personal view makes this framework powerful for us as individual leaders, whether on the front line or in the C-suite, as we deal with the daily challenges and uncertainties of leading. Once you understand the basics of this framework, you will have a new, more accurate map to help you navigate your work and lead in the most effective ways. This chapter will not make you an expert in the Cynefin Framework (there are resources to help you with that in the suggested reading list), but you don't need to be able to build a map to read and use one.

This framework will give you a new way of seeing and making sense of your world (so you can act with greater confidence even in the face of uncertainty). Flexible Leadership isn't solely based on the Cynefin Framework, but having this map will provide context and depth to our approach.

UNDERSTANDING THE FRAMEWORK

Donald Rumsfeld, while secretary of state under George W. Bush, in response to a question during a briefing about the lack of evidence linking Iraq to supplying terrorists with weapons of mass destruction, famously said:

> As we know, there are known knowns; there are things we know we know. We also know there are known unknowns; that is to say we know there are some things we do not know. But there are also unknown unknowns—the ones we don't know we don't know.[10]

The statement was a popular source for late-night comedians and doesn't sound very elegant. But the Cynefin Framework helps us see all three of those states Rumsfeld describes and adds one more. Here are the four major contexts, as described by the framework:

COMPLEX

Probe → Sense → Respond

Enabling Constraints

Exaptive Practice

COMPLICATED

Sense → Analyze → Respond

Governing Constraints

Good Practice

CHAOTIC

Act → Sense → Respond

No Effective Constraints

Novel Practice

CLEAR

Sense → Categorize → Respond

Fixed Constraints

Best Practice

Clear Context

This is the context of the known knowns. This is when we have simple cause-and-effect relationships that are easily seen. In this context, right answers rule, because everyone can see the same things and come to the same conclusions. In these situations, we can confidently measure, monitor, and manage. Most heavily process-oriented situations have a Clear context—order processing, inventory, auditing, and the manufacturing assembly line are all examples.

When we are in this context, our ability to recognize patterns serves us well. We can assess and categorize the situation and then respond based on *best practices*. We sense a solution, categorize it effectively based on examples and patterns, and then respond confidently (*sense – categorize – respond*).

Note that I italicized the phrase *best practices*. Why? Because in Clear context situations, applying best practices makes sense. We can define them (or define them with our team), and then apply those practices based on the analysis and categorization. It is in the obvious (or simple) and stable "black and white" situations where best practices reign supreme.

While this context seems, well, clear, there are still problems we can encounter because, here, we tend to rely on our existing thinking patterns. Here are four potential problems:

- *We oversimplify.* When we do this, we may miss unknowns and may get poor or unexpected results from our "best practices." Why? Because the practices don't match reality! If you are a leader who often asks for the highlights or the "TLDR" (i.e., "too long; didn't read"), you may risk the problem of

28

oversimplification. Remember, there is a difference between simple and simplistic.

- *We develop blind spots.* Our best practices, experience, training, and frequent success can blind us to new ways of thinking or keep us from looking closely enough. We sense the situation and categorize it too quickly, leading us to poor decisions with unintended consequences.

- *We get complacent.* My dad often said, "Always and never are a long time." It's bad grammar but a good reminder. If the context changes ("It's always been that way"), and we don't notice it, we make bad decisions. If you aren't sure what I mean, ask leaders at Blockbuster, Kodak, or most taxi companies. If you want to see what might be changing, listen more to those doing the work. They will see changes long before you will.

- *We rely on the status quo.* Best practices were developed in the past (maybe we should call them "past best practices"?). This means we risk relying on them even after the context has shifted. As helpful as these practices are in a situation with a Clear context, they become dangerous when the context changes and we don't change with it.

The Clear context is where we are (understandably) most comfortable, and likely you navigate within this context well—in fact, your skill at this likely was one reason you were promoted (recently or long ago) to being a manager or leader.

Unfortunately, this Clear context doesn't describe most of our work and the situations we experience every day. If it did, we wouldn't need this book.

Complicated Context

This is the context of the known unknowns. Here there is still a clear cause-and-effect relationship in the situation you are facing, but it takes expertise to see it. A singular right answer might not exist, but several good answers will. In a Complicated context, we must fight the urge to categorize, and rather analyze the possible solutions. So, instead of categorizing before responding, as in a Clear context, here we must analyze before making immediate conclusions (*sense – analyze – respond*). This analysis will likely find multiple good answers, often aided by expert help, all along a continuum of possibilities.

Consider deciding on the functionality of a new product. When considering three or more possible features, there are likely several combinations that could be desirable. Trying to determine a singular best combination may not be possible. In Complicated contexts, identifying or finding these options creates a range of good practices all worthy of consideration.

There are problems or challenges to existing thinking patterns here too. Here are three to be aware of and sidestep:

- *Beware the expert.* People with expertise are helpful in this context because they can do the analysis more clearly and effectively—until they can't. Ingrained thinking, ego, and past success may lead them to reject nontraditional or new views. If *you* are the expert, actively seek other inputs. If you are leading the experts, make time and space for dissenting ideas.
- *Beware the paralysis of analysis.* If we believe the context is Clear, or perhaps overly rely on our habits, we may spend too much time trying to find the best answer or practice rather than simply considering the range of good options available to us.

- *Beware the squelching of the nonexperts.* If those outside the expert circle (or whose expertise isn't valued) aren't heard, or don't feel it is safe to share, we risk sliding to an assumption that the context is Clear and simple. History gives us plenty of examples of experts predicting and deciding based on the assumption that everything is known. The nonexperts are often more likely to suggest the unknowns that shift us from simply categorizing and toward more analysis of the possible options.

Reaching decisions in the Complicated context can be time consuming and frustrating for most people. It involves trade-offs between trying to find the elusive right answer and "deciding and getting on with it." When we find ourselves struggling with this trade-off, remember that there are things we know are unknown. Realizing this, it is easier to step back from searching for the right answer and focus on comparing our available alternatives.

Complex Context

This is the context of the unknown unknowns. This is the domain Rumsfeld was speaking of in 2002, though ridiculed by many. While there were complex situations then, more and more business happens in this context today. But how is the complex actually different from the complicated?

Consider the difference between the computer I am writing these words on and the pet you might have in your house. Experts (not me) can dissemble this laptop, replace its parts, and put it back together, and it will work just fine. But your Max, Bella, Kitty, or Simba isn't a machine. These pets are complicated organisms, based on multiple inputs that interact in many ways. Your kitty, puppy, or parakeet is in a constant state of change. All these inputs, environmental factors, and antecedents combine to create a whole far greater than the sum of their lovable parts.

Most decisions in your business are complex because when one thing changes, there are many dominoes that fall, and all sorts of outcomes occur—unpredictable, many unintended, some unexpected, and not all desirable. For example, while we might believe a merger will create desirable results, not all the results will be so wonderful when viewed from a variety of perspectives (the uncertainty it creates being just one). When a policy to establish a certain number of days teams are to work in the office is created, it might seem straightforward. But your organization is more "organism" than it is machine, and many who have created these policies have found the context of that decision wasn't Clear or even Complicated but Complex in nature.

This is leading in a world of not knowing what we don't know. This truly is complex, as the Cynefin Framework defines it. The framework suggests our approach here as *probe – sense – respond*. To probe is to test, try, and then see what we learn from each iteration of experiments. In this context (and remember, this is where you and your team are working much of the time), best practices won't work, and good practices might not either. The focus is finding practices that emerge from your probing and testing that *might* work, or will at least improve your chances of working. That's why the Cynefin Framework suggests this is the context of *emergent practices*.

This context is challenging, and chances are you are knowingly nodding your head as you read about it. But there are common mistakes that our thinking patterns (and egos) might lead us to make here too. Here are two, with some suggestions for overcoming them:

- *Focus on taking control.* The desire to make progress may lead us to revert to (or slide toward) more traditional command-and-control approaches. If we don't recognize the situation is complicated, we may become impatient and lean even further toward leading via control. When we find ourselves moving in that direction, we must ask ourselves where we are on the map. By trying to force clarity where it doesn't exist and ignoring the testing and probing that complexity demands, we get suboptimal results and reduced engagement from the team. While neither of these is our goal when we are in the Complicated context, we often can't see how things will unfold, except with our 20/20 retrospective glasses on.

- *Focus on creating policies.* Policies work well in the Clear context. In those cases, there is a right answer, we find it and we codify it, and the policy works. Further, we know how to write and implement policies, and they create a sense of certainty and prove that we are acting. But everyone has seen policies go sideways and create unintended consequences. When the context is Complicated (and even Complex), the value of the seductive policy is diminished. In Complicated contexts, think *pilot*, not policy. In piloting and testing things, you will learn much more about the complicated situation you are in, and emergent practices will be revealed.

Since this is a context we live in more than we might have previously realized, it is where Flexible Leaders can shine. You will get far more familiar with this area and how we can more effectively respond to it throughout this book.

Chaotic Context

In the Chaotic context, the unknowns aren't just unknown—they are often unknowable. Searching for right answers in this case is pointless—because the cause and effect impacts on the situation you face can't be determined and both may be rapidly changing. Think about a massive explosion at your plant. Think of a hurricane approaching, where the path and strength are unknown and predictions keep evolving. Think September 11, 2001.

In these moments of high turbulence and chaos, we need to act. Here is where we can consider some other words from my dad: "Do something even if it is wrong." In the other contexts, this is bad advice. In Chaos, however, it creates a known state and provides a sense of order that gives us a foothold in the situation. Someone (likely us as leaders) needs to respond, communicate, and do so quickly and without input. This is the context where you can apply what you have learned about managing crisis situations.

But (and this is a big *but*) while the number of situations we will experience that are in a truly Chaotic context are rare, much of what has been extolled as great leadership practice happened within this rare context.

We value leaders who are decisive and act.

We value leaders who take risks.

We value leaders who can take charge.

Even those who focus on a more facilitative approach to leading know that these "take charge" factors matter. They are in our history books, our movies, and our stories. That view of leadership is a significant part of Western culture. There is nothing wrong with those attributes—when used in the right situations.

But a wiser, more self-aware Flexible Leader knows there is a time and place for these skills and habits. That time is when we are in Chaos.

I hope the Cynefin Framework opens your thinking and perspective (there is much more about how to use this map, starting in chapter 5). It is meant to be a map to help us navigate uncertainty.

But please don't lose the big idea in this new worldview. This framework, this map, helps us see that as leaders we must develop the skill of contextual response—we must get better at responding and leading based on actual context of a situation rather than based on habit, auto-responses, or intuition. Flexible Leaders build that skill, even though many of our human instincts want to create certainty and consider our working life in the Clear context even when it isn't.

PAUSE AND REFLECT

Before you move on, take a minute to think about these questions. (Even better if you take some notes on your thoughts!)

- What is the biggest idea I gained from this chapter?
- Which context do I think most of my work is in?
- How do I know?
- In which context am I most comfortable?
- Have I got the pronunciation of *Cynefin* (ku-*nev*-in) right in my head yet? (If not, repeat it a few times now—it rhymes with Kevin!)

> Sensemaking is: How do we make sense of the world so that we can act in it?

CHAPTER 3

HOW FLEXIBLE LEADERS THINK

Be careful how you think; your life is shaped by your thoughts.

—Proverbs 4:23 (Good News Translation)

Busyness is the bane of effective leaders. When we live in busy, we are so focused on activity, on the next task and the next fire, that we don't make or take or carve out the time . . .

   . . . to survey.

   . . . to navigate.

   . . . to strategize.

   . . . to learn.

   . . . to test.

   . . . to plan.

   . . . to ponder.

   . . . to think.

And as a Flexible Leader, this time is critical. Because without it we will . . .

. . . rely on habits.

. . . rely on our style.

. . . operate on autopilot.

And we need to make the time not only to think but also to understand some patterns and approaches to thinking that will serve us best. Why?

Because our thoughts inform our actions.

Better thoughts = better actions = better results

The Cynefin Framework gives us one new way to think, but there are several other thinking approaches, patterns, and mindsets we need for us to be confident through the uncertainty as Flexible Leaders.

THE ORGANIZATION AS AN ORGANISM

As organizations grew larger than a handful of closely knit people, they came to be viewed as hierarchical/mechanical systems. Given that these organizations grew from military and, later, manufacturing roots, that made sense. But while there is value in seeing organizations in this way, seeing them only in this way can limit our thinking. When we view organizations as "things," it leads us to think and act in corresponding ways. This mechanical view is prevalent across today's society and organizations. Here are a few things we take for granted that are rooted in this view of organizations:

- *Organization charts.* If there is a hierarchy to organizations, we need a map to understand it. The org chart is that map.
- *Best practices.* As we have already seen, best practices are great when the context and causes and effects are Clear (which is not as common as we would like or wish).

- *Specific job descriptions.* Each piece of the car has a specific function. If each part works effectively, the car will be functional. If you replace the word *car* with *organization*, you see when specific job descriptions make sense.
- *Specialization of work.* In a mechanical view of the world, roles that are highly specialized and structured build efficiency.
- *Formal communication channels.* Communication will be more efficient if it flows based on the hierarchy. This is another outcome and use of the org chart.

I am not saying that anything is completely wrong with these things, and in the mechanical view of organizational work, they make sense. Yet you have experienced frustrations or seen problems with each of these in your career.

What if we viewed organizations as living things instead—organisms rather than machines?

The concept of an organization as a living organism is a powerful alternative metaphor that isn't new. While you could trace the roots back 500 years, the dual construct of mechanistic and organismic structures primarily stems from the work of Tom Burns and George Stalker in the 1960s. They claimed that "a mechanistic management system is appropriate to stable conditions" whereas an *"organismic form is appropriate to changing conditions, which give rise constantly to fresh problems and unforeseen requirements* for action which cannot be broken down or distributed automatically arising from the functional roles defined with a hierarchic structure."[11] (Italics are mine.)

They wrote those words in the 1960s, but don't the italicized words sound like the world you work and lead in today?

Burns and Stalker suggested an "either/or" view of organizations: that they are either mechanistic *or* organismic. But the view of organizations as organisms hasn't gained widespread adoption societally, in organizations, or by leaders themselves. In this way, it seems that the duality (either/or) suggested by Burns and Stalker is limited. Instead, I suggest we can consider *both* metaphors helpful in understanding organizations.

What does the metaphor of your organization as a living thing teach us? Here are three suggestions:

- *Organizations can adapt.* Organizations can adapt and thrive in changing environments like living things. Whether those changes are drastic (think global pandemics) or more fleeting (like a major weather event), organizations can adjust, and the healthiest ones do.
- *Culture as organizational DNA.* All living things have DNA that determine their unique characteristics and abilities, and organizations have unique cultures that do the same. Every animal in a species is like the others, yet also unique. If you have ever walked from one department to another, one crew to another, or one office to another, you have seen the same phenomenon.
- *Teams experience life cycles.* Many have created models to describe the life cycle development of teams. These models all try to describe how teams and organizations go through stages of growth and development—which is clearly a biological, not mechanical, view.

These all seem familiar to you, I'm sure.

I've described a paradox—are organizations machines or organisms? From our short discussion, the answer is both! This is an example of something we need to wrestle with as Flexible Leaders. Consider this as a preview of things to come.

HOW TO THINK ABOUT CHANGE

In the 1860s, physician Claude Bernard had an important insight. As he studied the human body, he proposed that health is described by stability. Over 60 years later, scientist Walter Cannon gave this insight a name: homeostasis.

Homeostasis is the combination of two Greek words (*homoios* and *stasis*) that, literally translated, means "similar (or same) standing." Biologically, this means that living systems tend to resist change to maintain or continue in a stable state. As Brad Stulberg notes in his book *Master of Change: How to Excel When Everything Is Changing— Including You*, "homeostasis describes a cycle of order, disorder, and order."[12] Things are stable, then something happens to disrupt the system and create uncertainty, and the system strives to return to stability as quickly as possible.

This scientific insight has come to dominate how we think about change personally and organizationally. It is simple and seems to make sense. Generally speaking, it leads us to consider change as something to recover from, avoid if possible, and resist, and if it is inevitable, we strive to return to normal as fast as possible.

But what if we considered change from the perspective of another, newer scientific concept? In the 1980s, neuroscientist Peter Sterling and biologist Joseph Eyer observed something different than homeostasis. They noted that in many situations healthy systems do not automatically resist change but instead adapt to it. The observation applies to an organization shifting direction based on changes in their industry or an individual adjusting to the changes that come in various life stages. Sterling and Eyer called this phenomenon *allostasis* (meaning "variable standing" in Greek) and defined it as "stability through change."[13]

Homeostasis suggests we fight change and try to return to the previous status quo. Allostasis suggests that systems desire stability but that it can be found in a new normal—a new stability brought about by a change.

The COVID-19 pandemic gives us an interesting example to consider in relationship to these two ideas. At the start of 2020, we had a relatively stable global system of work. Then the virus happened. That created massive disorder and uncertainty in many things related to work practices, locations, times, and expectations.

What organizations did next revealed whether they were thinking homeostatically or allostatically.

Some organizations wanted to "get things back to normal" as quickly as possible. Many continued to announce new "return to office" dates, even as those timelines slipped. These were among the first to return to full office staffing. History shows that approach has caused even more uncertainty and unintended consequences. All because of an understandable desire to create stability—and wanting to find it in ways that have "always worked."

But other organizations took a different approach. While they faced the same change and wanted the same stability for their organizations and people, they didn't assume it would (or could) go back to the way it was before. With allostasis thinking (even if they had never heard of the term), they focused less on getting back to normal and more on creating a new normal. These organizations relooked at working schedules (times of day and/or days of the week), allowed hybrid or completely remote working arrangements, and recruited from a wider geographic footprint. They took the same uncertainty and disorder as a chance to learn, grow, and adapt.

When you see allostasis (strength through change) as a possible mindset, it will make it far easier for you to recognize, value, and navigate through the contexts of the Cynefin Framework. As a bonus, you will be more effective in understanding and leading change.

THE POWER OF PARADOX: BOTH/AND THINKING

The Cynefin Framework shows us what we already knew, though we may not have had words for it. The context of the world we live and work in isn't always Clear. When things are Complex or Complicated, we can't think in black or white, right or wrong, or either/or ways. In those (frequent) situations, as leaders we must be willing, able, and confident in thinking in paradoxes, seeing shades of gray, considering trade-offs, and thinking both/and.

F. Scott Fitzgerald wrote, "The test of a first-rate intelligence is the ability to hold two opposing ideas in mind at the same time and still retain the ability to function. One should, for example, be able to see that things are hopeless yet be determined to make them otherwise."[14]

If we want to be wise, capable, and flexible leaders, we need to be able to see the tensions in situations and make decisions in a world of paradox.

Wendy K. Smith and Marianne W. Lewis, in their wonderful book *Both/And Thinking: Embracing Creative Tensions to Solve Your Toughest Problems*, frame it this way: "Developing both/and thinking begins by starting to notice the paradoxes that lurk beneath our presenting dilemmas. The next step involves us learning to more effectively navigate those paradoxes."[15]

They suggest four types of paradoxes, as shown in the following image.

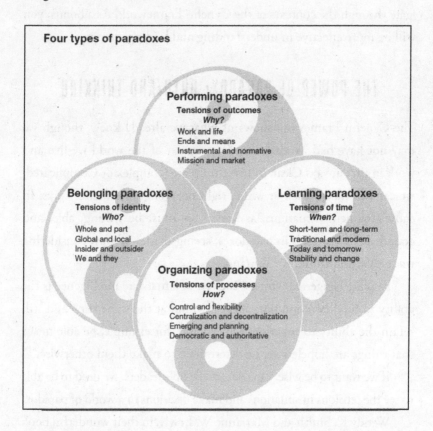

Four types of paradoxes

Performing paradoxes
Tensions of outcomes
Why?
Work and life
Ends and means
Instrumental and normative
Mission and market

Belonging paradoxes
Tensions of identity
Who?
Whole and part
Global and local
Insider and outsider
We and they

Learning paradoxes
Tensions of time
When?
Short-term and long-term
Traditional and modern
Today and tomorrow
Stability and change

Organizing paradoxes
Tensions of processes
How?
Control and flexibility
Centralization and decentralization
Emerging and planning
Democratic and authoritative

You will leave this book with examples of how a Flexible Leader can understand and lead through each of these types of paradoxes.

THREE TYPES OF REASONING

In school we learned about two kinds of reasoning: deductive and inductive. But since it may have been a while, and you likely didn't take philosophy in college, let's review.

Deductive reasoning is when we draw conclusions from rules. If the rule is that Christmas is always December 25, and we know that today is December 25, we deduce that today must be Christmas. Deductive reasoning allows us to reach a conclusion that:

- starts with a general statement of truth
- is logical—it "makes sense"
- is true—it is based on facts
- is valid—when you compare the first condition with the second, your decision is well grounded

You can think about it this way—in deductive reasoning:

General rule → Specific Conclusion

The good news is that if the rule is correct, the conclusion will be too. But if the rules are misapplied or no longer are true, the conclusion will be faulty.

Inductive reasoning starts not with a general rule but with a specific observation. The goal is to use the information you have to draw a general conclusion. If three customers call in with problems with your website, it is likely the bulk of your incoming calls will be about your website until it gets fixed.

You can think about it this way—in inductive reasoning:

Specific Observation → General Conclusion

The observations may lead to a true conclusion, but there is no guarantee.

While you have probably heard of both deductive and inductive reasoning, you may have forgotten about the third kind: abductive reasoning. It seems to lead to less certain results, which may be why it isn't talked about as much. But in a world of uncertainty and when we are often in Complex and Complicated contexts, it becomes super useful.

Abductive reasoning looks at a few observations (that are likely or known to be incomplete) and creates an explanation. You might think of this as a hunch from which we create a belief. Netflix observed that their customers were frustrated by DVD late fees and drew the conclusion that people wanted an easier way to return their DVD rentals—without those fees. As a result, they created a subscription-based service that offered customers an easier way to return their rentals. Without that reasoning, there likely wouldn't have been a business that they could eventually pivot to a streaming service.

You can think about it this way—in abductive reasoning:

Incomplete Observations → Prediction or Guess

Becoming comfortable with this sort of reasoning in a world where we can observe plenty but not often see the whole picture is a critical skill for Flexible Leaders.

THINKING FAST AND SLOW

Daniel Kahneman's classic *Thinking, Fast and Slow*[16] can't be summarized in full here. Over nearly 500 pages, Kahneman unveils example after example of our biases, our heuristics, how they happen, and why they are problematic. While it is long, I highly recommend this book as a source to understand not only how we think, but also how our teams, teammates, customers, vendors, and even organizations think.

For our specific purposes, we need to understand the "main characters" of our thinking.

Kahneman suggests our brains have two characters: System 1, which thinks fast, and System 2, which thinks slow.

System 1 thinks on autopilot, reacts intuitively, and requires little effort. If someone asks you your name, System 1 takes over. When you respond to a situation at work based on your "leadership style," System 1 gets you there. When you are doing a task you know well, like brushing your teeth, driving, or completing that SOP at work, System 1 is at work.

System 2 requires us to slow down, to deliberate, to focus and concentrate, or to consider more data. If you are solving a problem you know is complex, System 2 is ready. When you are completing performance reviews, you lean into System 2 (I hope). When you are determining what your next car should be, you likely rely on System 2 thinking.

We use both systems every day and need both to be successful in life. Unfortunately, System 1 operates on heuristics, or shortcuts, which aren't always accurate (for instance, we may falsely assume the context of our situation is Clear). If we want to move past what is automatic, we need System 2 thinking. Unfortunately, System 2 thinking not only takes more time but is also harder work! Kahneman's work helps us "recognize situations in which mistakes are likely and try harder to avoid significant mistakes when stakes are high." (Doesn't this sound like your job?)

Since the stakes are often high and the context isn't always Clear for us as leaders, being willing (and knowing how and when) to shift to System 2 thinking is a critical part of being a Flexible Leader.

FINAL THOUGHTS

I know you might be thinking, *Kevin, get on with the skills—what do I need to do to become a Flexible Leader?* If you are thinking that, let me just say that while I understand that sentiment:

- Remember that being a Flexible Leader is in part about creating wisdom and cognitive flexibility, so a little patience is good practice.
- Realize you already have new tools for navigation and thinking in your tool kit.
- Remember that taking the time to gain tools for thinking more clearly will help you build your skills more quickly and consistently.
- Note that until mindset and skillset are aligned, you will never build the habitset of a successful Flexible Leader.

Having said that, we now have the mindset tools we need, so let's build some Flexible Leadership skills.

PAUSE AND REFLECT

Before you move on, take a minute to think about these questions. (Even better if you take some notes on your thoughts!)

- Which ideas or mindsets in this chapter are most helpful to me?
- How can I apply them in my work right now?

> Remember that taking the time to gain tools for thinking more clearly will help you build your skills more quickly and consistently.

THE SKILLSET OF FLEXIBLE LEADERS

> The best leaders don't know just one style of leadership—
> they're skilled at several, and have the flexibility to switch
> between styles as the circumstance dictates.
>
> —Daniel Goleman, author

We spent the first section of this book creating the whys, needs, and mindset of Flexible Leaders. Now it's time to learn the process and skills that will allow us to become more Flexible Leaders. I'll describe the Flexible Leadership Approach, which includes three parts:

- Intention
- Context
- Flexors

Intention + Context + Flexors = Flexible Leadership

If you were hoping there wouldn't be any math here, don't worry. This formula is metaphorical and meant to help us see and remember the key components of Flexible Leadership. If we were to put numbers into this formula, we would quickly see that the greater the value of each component, the bigger the value of the result. Since our goal is to become more flexible leaders, we must focus on each of these components and work to use them more effectively.

$$1 + 1 + 1 < 2 + 2 + 2$$

While math would say we can get to the same resulting level of Flexible Leadership success in a variety of ways . . .

$$1 + 1 + 1 = 3$$

$$1 + 2 + 0 = 3$$

$$3 + 0 + 0 = 3$$

. . . can you really become a more flexible leader without using all three components well (or equally)?

The math says you can move in the direction of greater flexibility and effectiveness if you lean into one of the components at the expense of or by ignoring another. But that isn't very likely in reality. Reaching the level of impact that you want and that your team and organization needs requires us to look at, understand, and apply each of these components. More of each is better, but you maximize the Flexible Leadership Approach when all three are being effectively used. Let's talk about each of the components of the Flexible Leadership Approach in the next four chapters.

CHAPTER 4

INTENTION

You create your thoughts, your thoughts create your intentions, and your intentions create your reality.

—Wayne Dyer, author[17]

The Flexible Leadership Approach we are exploring isn't natural. While some parts of what you have read may already influence how you think and lead, becoming a more flexible leader requires us to move past several mental and habitual barriers.

Thinking differently requires us to understand how we do think, what the other options might be, and the benefits of those new approaches and perspectives.

Overriding our habits involves suspending our automatic responses to specific situations. This isn't easy, especially when those habits seem like they have helped us succeed to this point. Doing this is hard work. We can only override the automatic with a decision—an intention—to do it.

Overcoming our automatic thoughts and understood patterns and responses requires:

- awareness of the limitations of our current approaches
- examples of other options
- knowledge of what got us to our current habit
- a desire to create new patterns or habits
- a willingness to try something different
- triggers to stop the auto responses
- an intention to stop the auto responses and choose new ones

Since becoming a Flexible Leader isn't natural, intention will be critical to your success. Without the intention to be more flexible, you won't do the observation and thinking work required, and you won't become as flexible, adaptable, resilient, and effective as you possibly could. Note, too, that while experience as a leader can be helpful in many ways, when it comes to being a more flexible leader, it can get in your way.

Why? Because the longer you have been leading, the more habits and auto-responses you have—making a new intention even more important.

As your personal experience likely tells you, willpower and desire aren't enough. If you want to understand more about the process of habit change in general, there are several great books on the subject, including the long-popular (and excellent) *Atomic Habits* by James Clear. (We will talk more about that book as it specifically relates to Flexible Leadership in chapter 12.)

Let's talk about each of the requirements listed in more detail.

Awareness of Limitations

If you aren't aware that you could be a more effective leader who could be making a bigger impact, you wouldn't be reading this book. While I don't know where you see that gap, I know you have enough awareness to choose intentionality.

Examples of Options

Awareness isn't enough. We can know that what we are doing isn't working as well as we would like, but if we don't know what we could do instead, we are stuck. One of the goals of this book is to help you see options you might not have considered before and help you understand why you might be stuck. Which leads to . . .

Knowledge of What Got Us Here

In my experience in working with and observing leaders, a lack of this knowledge is a significant barrier to the intention to make any changes to existing patterns and behaviors. There are four specific thinking biases that hurt us here.

- *Experience bias.* We rely on our experience to make judgments. We interpret the past to help us move into the future. This makes sense because we have been successful to this point, haven't we? Unfortunately, we can overvalue our experience and put ourselves at the center of our mental universe at the same time. (All humans do this, but, hey, we are the boss, so we are supposed to know and have been chosen to lead—ultimately making the risk greater for us.) Experience bias leads us to assume our view of the problem or situation is the complete picture. At this point, it should be obvious that is seldom correct.
- *Confirmation bias.* Confirmation bias is our tendency to look for (or only see) information that aligns with our previously held views, and it ignores contrary information or input. Putting this together with experience bias leaves us feeling pretty

good about our decisions and approaches—and keeps us from trying (or even considering) anything different.

- *Personal labels and stereotypes.* One reason we don't consider changing, adapting, or being more flexible is the labels we have placed on ourselves. If you label yourself as poor at math, you will avoid math when possible (and your confidence in the subject and skills will be affected as well). If you consider yourself unorganized, you may not like your messy desk, but you can justify it. Similarly, in leadership, if you have taken any sort of style assessment—whether behavioral, strengths, communication, or leadership—you may succumb to this blind spot. "I'm an INFP, so I lead this way." "I have these strengths, so . . ." "I am a collaborative leader, so . . ." As helpful as these models and assessments can be, they are necessarily oversimplified to real life. And the unintended consequence of this "understanding" is that we label ourselves—both justifying our behavior and resigning ourselves to that belief. We know that stereotyping others is dangerous. But we don't always see how much we limit ourselves with our personal labels.

- *Pattern recognition.* When making decisions, we use many internal tools—multiple senses, information (old and new), and our previous experience. Pattern recognition comes when we realize we've made the same decision before. So, rather than making a new analysis, we reference our catalog of previous decisions. For example, we see large, flat, upright pieces of wood or steel attached to buildings as doors. Because we have used or seen them used before, we know what they are for and how they work. We open and close them to enter and exit locations. That knowledge comes from our personal knowledge base or experience, and reusing the same knowledge or experience creates the pattern. It would be hard to navigate our world without the power of pattern recognition, but it also impedes us from becoming more flexible leaders because it leads to oversimplifying a complex situation, misinterpreting a situation, or relying on confirmation bias.

All of these thinking patterns create blind spots. If we don't know or see them and the problems they can cause, how can we change?

We can overcome all of these human tendencies, but not until we are aware of them. Ask yourself which of these thinking patterns get in your way. Better yet, ask someone you trust and who knows you well which ones they see in you.

Desire to Change

The comfort zone, where we have little or no dissatisfaction with the way things are, is a big impediment to change. You could have all the pieces so far but still say, "So what? It doesn't matter. I'm happy with the way I lead and the results I get." If there is no desire to change your habits as a leader, it is very likely no change will occur. No desire to change means no intentional consideration of the actions that lead to Flexible Leadership. If you are still reading, chances are this one isn't your challenge—you know that change can mean improvement, and it is improvement you desire. While we need to create or nurture a desire to change in ourselves, this is a challenge as we lead others too. Whether for yourself or others, if the desire is weak or nonexistent, focus on more clearly seeing (or helping others see) the positives in a changed future. A desire to change (that is, a dissatisfaction with our current state) grows as our vision of a desired future becomes clearer.

Willingness to Change

Desire is critical but not enough on its own either. If there is no willingness to create change (or belief that you are capable of doing so), you will remain in your existing thinking and behavioral habits and patterns. Earlier in the book, we talked about the importance of confidence. One of my biggest goals for this book is that you leave with the confidence and willingness to try, apply, and succeed with these Flexible Leadership principles and approaches.

Triggers

It is one thing to know that you *could* do something other than what comes naturally or automatically, but it is another thing to know *when* you need to override that conditioned response! The good news is that in the other two components of the Flexible Leadership Approach, you see when you need to pause, consider, and perhaps act differently than you would have automatically. We will explore this more in chapter 9.

———

When these markers of intention we just reviewed are in place, we can actively and intentionally resist our natural tendencies, styles, preexisting beliefs, and patterns. With intention, we are on the path to being more flexible leaders.

An important side note: Reread this entire section, thinking about one or more of your team members. Consider how each of these components relates to their willingness and capability to implement any coaching you provide. Think about something you would like to help them change or improve. Can they or will they apply that feedback or make that change without clear intention?

It is important to realize that the best coaches help those they coach build this intention. When intention is missing, old habits and existing patterns always win. And that means your results will lose.

PAUSE AND REFLECT

Before you move on, take a minute to think about these questions. (Even better if you take some notes on your thoughts!)

- Which of these barriers most often get in the way of my making intentional change?
- Which of these do I need to most overcome to intentionally work on being a more flexible leader?

We know that stereotyping others is dangerous. But we don't always see how much we limit ourselves with our personal labels.

CHAPTER 5

CONTEXT

Taken out of context, I must seem so strange.

—Ani DiFranco, singer-songwriter[18]

The second component of the formula is context.

To help us make sense of the context we are leading in, whether leading a team meeting, outlining the need to solve a problem, championing a change (whether one you initiated or not), or building strategies for the global expansion of our enterprise, we will use the Cynefin Framework we've already explored. Let's explore how we can use this framework as our Context Map.

When we look at a problem or situation like any of those shown in the framework on page 60 (or a thousand more), our experience says we need to look at the options, pick one, and then execute on that option. We do this all the time—consciously or not. But this approach assumes we can determine the cause of the situation, which means we can delineate or determine the effects from those causes.

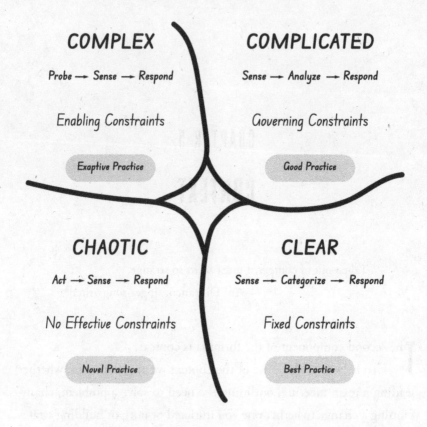

COMPLEX

Probe → Sense → Respond

Enabling Constraints

Exaptive Practice

COMPLICATED

Sense → Analyze → Respond

Governing Constraints

Good Practice

CHAOTIC

Act → Sense → Respond

No Effective Constraints

Novel Practice

CLEAR

Sense → Categorize → Respond

Fixed Constraints

Best Practice

If we do X, we have a good idea that Y will happen because we know the underlying cause. In other words, we operate assuming the context of the situation is Clear or Complicated (on the right side of the map). If cause and effect is obvious or can be determined, and there is some order to the system you are leading in, this is exactly where you should start.

But not all systems are ordered—we can't always determine the cause-and-effect relationship that exists, and sometimes causality can only be determined in hindsight. These are the situations on the left side of the map. Think of the times you've looked back and seen why things worked out the way they did, or why people responded the way they did, and realized you had no way of knowing that beforehand.

Here is another tangible example of the difference between ordered and unordered systems, from Greg Brougham in his book *The Cynefin Mini-Book: An Introduction to Complexity and the Cynefin Framework*: "Systems that are ordered . . . we can take apart and put back together again—for example a car or aero-plane; those that are un-ordered can never be deconstructed then put back together. For example, think of making mayonnaise."[19]

How many of the situations (contexts) that you find yourself in as a leader look more like mayonnaise than a car? (And do you see the machine/organism paradox here again too?)

To a Flexible Leader, context means being able to determine the underlying nature of our situation—where we are on the map. Let me give you two starting points to help you find the right context on the map.

Ask yourself these questions:

1. Have you seen this before or do you have any relevant experience? If so, you are likely in an ordered system and can start on the right side of the map.
2. Does this look novel or not quite like anything you've seen before? If so, you are likely in an unordered system and can start on the left side of the map.

If you can decide on ordered versus unordered but aren't sure of the specific context, consider the worse of the two options—meaning, assume Complicated, not Clear, and Chaotic, not Complex. This will counteract our tendency to oversimplify and fool ourselves into knowing the answer already!

Here is a slightly more specific description of our map that helps decide what to do once we know where we are located:

UNORDERED   ORDERED

COMPLEX

- There are unknown unknowns
- Competing ideas and opinions exist
- Things are unpredictable and unstable
- Paradox and contradictions exist
- Need for ideas and innovation

COMPLICATED

- There are knowns and unknowns
- We can forecast or guess but it is hard to definitely know
- Experts are needed
- Situational analysis needed

CHAOTIC

- There are unknowables!
- High turbulence and tension
- No patterns seem to exist
- No time to think
- Many decisions to make . . . now

CLEAR

- The knowns are known
- Familiar and known patterns
- Wide agreement on cause and effect
- We have the facts and they are indisputable
- Obvious and agreed-on solutions

Once you have the context determined, there are specific steps you can take. As you read these steps, think back to our discussion of intention in the last chapter. You may notice that only some of these actions are what you are used to doing, have confidence in doing, or have defined yourself as being able to do. Getting the context right sets the table for you to be able to flex your approach to meet the needs of the situation.

There are some proven general suggestions to help you navigate in whatever context you are in. But there are potential risks in each context too. Here are some suggestions and things to be aware of as you navigate each one.

If the Context Is Clear

Suggestions
- Create or follow best practices
- Focus on replication of proven methods
- Standardize processes
- Create effective and clear documentation
- Communicate clearly
- Delegate or share responsibility

Beware of . . .
- Complacency or too much sense of comfort
- Ignoring dissenting voices—something might be changing that we aren't seeing
- Not seeing warning signs of change
- Treating current best practices as evergreen or eternal
- Closed minds—of you or others in the system

If the Context Is Complicated

Suggestions
- Determine experts to help analyze the situation (whether across the team/organization or externally)
- Create space and opportunity for others to share their thoughts and ideas

- Based on analysis of the situation, consider more options
- Listen (much) more carefully
- Help people see the full context
- Consider shared decision-making

Beware of . . .

- Oversimplification
- Overconfident or dogmatic experts
- Blindly following expert opinions
- Not considering insights/ideas of "nonexperts"
- Paralysis of (over)analysis

If the Context Is Complex

Suggestions

- Look for a range of possible or plausible causes and solutions
- Increase the level of communication and exploration
- Rely less on past expertise and more on diversity of thought and perspectives
- Keep your mind and others' minds open longer
- Consider pilots and experiments and lower-risk testing
- Look for trends and patterns to emerge

Beware of . . .

- The temptation to take over and decide
- The desire to move too quickly

If the Context Is Chaotic

Suggestions

- Try things and see what you learn

- Act in a "command and control" approach to leadership
- Communicate clearly, directly, and quickly
- Focus on getting out of Chaos and back to Complex

Beware of . . .
- Staying in "command and control" too long (when the situation is no longer Chaotic)
- Missing the chance for innovation as you stay with "one-off" actions
- Feeling you are indispensable

———

Now you have a map to help you more clearly see the situations you are working in. As I have said previously, without this map, too many leaders make one of two false assumptions:

1. *Most contexts are Clear.* Thirty years ago, in a less globally connected world with fewer interdependencies, this was truer than today. Though the world has become more complicated and complex (most would agree with that statement, even without our map), we haven't changed our approach to leading.
2. *We are living in Chaos!* The uncertainty we feel can make us assume we are in Chaos, but hopefully now with your new map you see that this is less often the actual case. The Chaotic context is likely the rarest one you will find yourself in during your career.

Since you are leading in uncharted waters, a map will help. Just like how a map of unfamiliar terrain helps an explorer get to their destination, this map will help you lead more effectively in the contexts you face.

PAUSE AND REFLECT

Before you move on, take a minute to think about these questions. (Even better if you take some notes on your thoughts!)

- Which of the contexts was the biggest eye-opener for me?
- Which one am I likely operating in more than I realized previously?

Getting the context right sets the table for you to be able to flex your approach to meet the needs of the situation.

CHAPTER 6

FLEXORS

The art of life lies in a constant readjustment to our
surroundings.

—Okakura Kakuzō, scholar and art critic[20]

We have talked about the desire and intention to flex our approach
and have a new way to think about the context of our situation.
Now we need to know about the actual adjustments to make. Introducing Flexors.

The way most people think about their approach to leadership is to
lean into their experience or the labels they gain from their style. Here's
a visual example from the 3O Model of Leadership.

Outcomes   Others

Some leaders focus on the outcomes required in a situation. They ask questions about what is needed, what the goals are, and the like. Others take a people-centric approach, believing that leaning into the needs and concerns of the team will ultimately get the outcomes they need. Since both approaches have value, yet we see them as opposing approaches, they create a paradox. While there is a paradox here, thinking about these as fully separate approaches also creates a *false dichotomy*.

To become more effective and flexible leaders, we need to think of these two approaches in tension with each other. In other words, we need to see them as a Flexor. A Flexor is a pair of (generally seen as opposing) possible approaches that Flexible Leaders see as symbiotic.

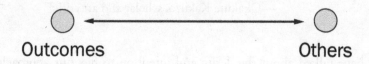

Outcomes   Others

This is the Outcomes/Others Flexor. There are times we need to focus on the outcomes and times where our focus might need to be more on others—those doing the work. Seeing these two approaches as a Flexor challenges us to both/and thinking. (Note: I am using this overarching Flexor as just one example. In future chapters, I will share 18 others with you.)

Using Flexors in each leadership situation forces us to move from using our preferred, natural, or learned approach to considering more choices. When we see the tension between the ends of the Flexor spectrum, we realize we can adjust our response based on the needs of the situation.

But it's not just seeing the ends—it is realizing something more profound. Choosing an end of the spectrum without considering the spectrum itself will rarely give us the best results.

An Example

Imagine your team is facing a significant production challenge. You are getting pressure from above (and/or from customers) to get more of a particular product out the door this month. The problem is urgent, and the pressure is real.

Based on your experience and inclination, you decide an outcome-focused approach is called for. So you call the team together and urge a hyper-focus on the production. You let people know, "We need to meet these quotas at all costs!" You authorize overtime as needed and personally become more invested and involved making sure the team hits those quotas. Maybe you hit those targets and the problem is solved, or maybe not. But there may be other consequences (even if they are unintended). The team might be confused by your micromanagement, and trust might be reduced. Burnout or mental health issues might arise (even if you don't notice them). You might even see an uptick in turnover—and maybe you won't even attribute it to the situation. Because, after all, the crisis was averted.

Or maybe . . .

Based on your experience and inclination, you decide an others-focused approach is called for. So you call the team together and explain the situation. You acknowledge that this might be a big challenge. You elicit their ideas as to the causes of the problem (especially if they aren't completely known) and get their thoughts on what the best courses of action are. You remind everyone how important it is to meet the production commitments and take care of the customers. You ask the team how you can best support them. Maybe you hit the target, or maybe you fall short. But there may be other consequences as well (even if they are unintended). You might have uncomfortable conversations with those above you if you miss the target. The team might further gel, gaining you advantages into the future. The team might identify root causes or process changes that keep this from being a recurring problem. Your culture may grow stronger and more resilient.

Or maybe . . .

You step back and consider your options. You realize that the outcome is important, but so are your people. So, rather than taking an approach that is 90–100% outcome focused or 90–100% other focused, you consider where your approach should be in the tension between the opposing ends of the spectrum. How far you lean toward outcomes or others, then, depends on the context of the situation, the relationships you have with your superiors and your team, and a hundred other factors. Taking this approach is what it means to be a Flexible Leader. Moving past your inclinations and experiences, styles, and self-talk to intentionally choose what to do based on the context and tension of the Flexor.

Flexor thinking reminds us that the right answers are rarely at the far ends of the spectrum, but rather somewhere in between. When we slow down enough to get past our habits, we can decide how to flex in a specific situation. Thinking in terms of Flexors allows you to consider what the right mix or balance in your approach could be rather than focusing on a single choice. Thinking and acting based on Flexors is key to becoming a more flexible leader.

PAUSE AND REFLECT

Before you move on, take a minute to think about these questions. (Even better if you take some notes on your thoughts!)

- How do I feel about this idea of Flexors?
- Where do I tend to lean on the Outcomes/Others Flexor?

Flexor thinking reminds us that the right answers are rarely at the far ends of the spectrum, but rather somewhere in between. When we slow down enough to get past our habits, we can decide how to flex in a specific situation.

CHAPTER 7

THE FLEXIBLE LEADERSHIP APPROACH

Fit no stereotypes. Don't chase the latest management fads. The situation dictates which approach best accomplishes the team's mission.

— Colin Powell, former US Secretary of State[21]

In the next chapter, we will explore specific Flexors and how to apply them. But for now, let's go back to the formula that constitutes the Flexible Leadership Approach.

Intention + Context + Flexors = Flexible Leadership

You won't become a Flexible Leader without intentionality. Without that, you will operate on autopilot. Sometimes your natural or learned approach will work; sometimes it won't. But if you don't want to play the lottery every day, you must intentionally choose the other two parts of the model.

When you understand the context of your situation, you are in a better position to decide how to proceed. While the context gives you a general starting point for your leadership actions for the specifics of your situation, it isn't enough. Knowing your location and having a compass is helpful if you are lost, but you still need to find the best path to lead you safely to your destination. As a Flexible Leader, that means you must think in terms of Flexors.

Flexors help you determine the right combination of mindsets and skillsets needed in this moment. And the choice might be different tomorrow or next week, depending on the context you are facing then.

Flexible Leadership isn't the easiest path, but as you get more adept at applying this approach, you will find it is the most effective long-term path.

An Example

Let's return to the example I shared in the last chapter:

Imagine your team is facing a significant production challenge. You are getting pressure from above (and/or from customers) to get more of a particular product out the door this month. The problem is urgent, and the pressure is real.

While intention will always be needed to overcome our natural tendencies, we need a way or a reason to stop long enough to turn off the autopilot response. There is more about this in the third section of the book, but for now let's look at the situation I've outlined. We see that the issue at hand is important and a big deal. This should be an obvious cue for us to realize that we may need to flex our approach. After all, your existing approaches may have contributed to this situation (sorry if you didn't want to hear that). When you get to this mental moment, congratulations—you now have the intention to consider new options and alternatives!

Next, you consider the context. By slowing down enough to do this, you can start to plan your path forward.

- If you determine the context is Clear (e.g., you have had a mechanical issue in the plant that got you behind), you can move forward based on knowing why the problem has occurred and what the proven resolution might be. Then you can apply the Outcomes/Others Flexor based on that. Now you can consider the levels of commitment and knowledge/experience of your team, as well as the trust that exists to determine how you will balance the Outcomes/Others Flexor.

- If you determine the context is Complicated (e.g., there is an ongoing challenge with a piece of production equipment failing and there are a variety of opinions as to why it is happening), you can start by gaining expert input. That may or may not exist within your team, but either way, rather than simply moving forward, you will slow down enough to determine the options you have. Even if you don't deem your team as having all the needed expertise, you can still realize they have some and give them space to contribute. Knowing that the context is Complicated means you will likely be flexing in the direction of others—to get input and commitment to a plan that has uncertainty involved.

- If you determine the context is Complex (e.g., you have some unclear supply issues and the sources of them aren't clear), you will likely flex toward others as well. You can ask the team to help you identify plausible causes of your production shortfall and some approaches that will address them.

- If you determine the context is Chaos (e.g., the plant has been down due to a tornado that damaged some of the building and disrupted the community), where you are being asked/expected to solve a particularly unusual situation with limited (or unknowable) information, you will likely need to act quickly. This means that even if your inclination might be to lean toward the others side of the Flexor, you need to try something *now*. In Chaotic situations, you will need to flex toward outcomes until the situation stabilizes. Then you might need to flex to a different spot on the spectrum.

Now you have the overall approach, an understanding of the components, and have seen an example. In other words, you have the basics of the Flexible Leadership Approach. In the next chapter we will begin taking a deep dive into the many different Flexors you can apply.

PAUSE AND REFLECT

Before you move on, take a minute to think about these questions. (Even better if you take some notes on your thoughts!)

- Now that I understand the Flexible Leadership Approach, which component excites me most?
- Where do I think I have the most need for growth?
- Which component will make the biggest impact for me and the team?
- Where will I start?

RESOURCES TO HELP YOU LEAD FLEXIBLY

You can get a pocket guide to using the sensemaking framework at FlexibleLeadershipBook.com or by scanning this QR code.

> You won't become a Flexible Leader without intentionality. Without that, you will operate on autopilot. Sometimes your natural or learned approach will work; sometimes it won't. But if you don't want to play the lottery every day, you must intentionally choose the other two parts of the model.

CHAPTER 8

THE BIG PICTURE FLEXORS

The boldness of asking deep questions may require unforeseen flexibility if we are to accept the answers.

—Brian Greene, physicist

Once you understand the mindset of Flexors, you begin to unlock the power of Flexible Leadership. The core idea is that there is almost always a range of approaches you can take on a spectrum of options, and that the best choice won't always be the same in every situation or our personal favorite. Finding the right course of action requires you to choose based on the situational needs you face.

Previously I introduced the Outcomes/Others Flexor. But it is far from the only one. This is the first of two chapters describing more Flexors. First we will explore the Big Picture Flexors. Consider these the overarching approaches that seem to guide our thinking and decision-making. You will begin to see the styles and identities you have ascribed to yourself in these. There will also be those that many of us are most prone to avoid, opting instead to just go with our style, strength, or natural inclination.

In these Flexor chapters, we'll look at the aspects of each specific Flexor, considering:

- The nature of the Flexor
- The impacts at the ends of the spectrum
- When to apply it
- How to decide
- An example to make your choices/actions more tangible

As you read about each of them, remember that the art of Flexible Leadership is acknowledging that success is rarely on the extreme ends of the Flexor spectrum and will usually lie somewhere between those extremes. Where it falls in the center band will depend on your intention and the context of the situation.

THE COMPLIANCE/COMMITMENT FLEXOR

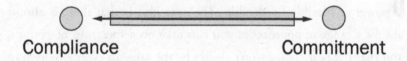

Compliance   Commitment

This is perhaps the biggest overarching Flexor of all, and your natural inclinations on this one likely say much about how you lead and how successful you are. Here is the question: *Would you rather lead for compliance or commitment?* Having asked hundreds of people this question in groups, I'm guessing your answer is the same as theirs . . .

You'd prefer commitment.

Yet many do not lead in ways that support that sentiment.

The Impacts at the Ends

Leading merely for compliance is the picture of the command-and-control "because I'm the boss and I said so" leader. When we lean into compliance, we will get results. People will say, "Yes, Boss," but we will, in most cases, get the bare minimum from them in effort, engagement, and input. Strict compliance will be situational and transactional. Maybe (and only maybe) that might be enough if people are digging a ditch. But the work of your team is more complex and integrated than one single, arbitrary task.

While you would likely opt for commitment, we can overdo this approach and goal too. If a leader is too focused on commitment, they may waste time or leave people frustrated. While people do want to have a say, be empowered, and be engaged, sometimes they are fine with us just deciding. Leaning too far into commitment may leave us searching for an answer that delights everyone when delight (or even agreement) might not be needed.

When to Apply It

In short, if the context is Chaotic, people need you to declare a goal, make a decision, and set a direction. When fire is lapping at the door, a hurricane is approaching your plant, or when we don't even know what we don't know, people will comply.

Just decide.

Try something.

Create a starting point.

In these moments, people want you to be in control mode and will likely be willing to follow. So leaning into compliance then is valuable, even more effective.

But as the Chaos eases, and the context looks more Complicated or Complex, you need to move (rapidly) toward the goal of building commitment.

How to Decide

Here are some ways to decide which direction to slide or lean on this Flexor.

Lean toward compliance when:
- the context is Clear, meaning there will likely be widespread agreement and understanding about the decision you communicate.
- things are Chaotic.
- time is short.
- the issue is short term in nature.
- people won't be significantly impacted by your decision-making (from their perspective, not yours).
- people aren't very invested in the issue (i.e., they don't care much whatever you decide and will go along).
- compliance won't lead to other unintended consequences.

Lean toward commitment when:
- the context is Complicated or Complex.
- people on your team or who are available to your team have expertise and relevant experience.
- people are more invested in the outcome.
- the implications of the issue or decision are long lasting.

- you don't have all the information you might need to make a decision alone.
- people see and care about the big picture.
- you have time to gather information, create dialogue, and build commitment.
- you can't afford not to have people committed.

Here's a visual simplification:

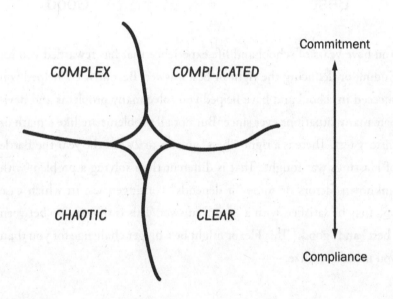

An Example

You are coaching someone and want them to change their behavior, performance, or results. You know it will take time, effort, and focus for them to make the change. You want the changed behavior or performance to be lasting. This is clearly a time when you want to lead and coach for the commitment of that person. You want them to see the value of the change and be willing to do what it takes for that lasting change to occur. These goals won't be reached if you take a directive, direct, and advice-heavy approach. If you simply want them to comply with your directive, you will need to lead in a way that elicits that compliance from them.

THE BEST/GOOD FLEXOR

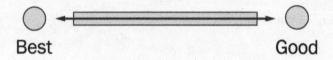

Best   Good

You have years of school and life experience that has rewarded you for finding or deducing the right or best answer. Best answers helped you succeed in school and have helped you solve many problems and navigate many situations ever since. But not all problems are like a math or history test. There is a right, "best" answer to 2+2 or the year the Battle of Hastings was fought. That is different than solving a problem with unknown factors or some "it depends" contingencies, in which case you may be satisfied with a "good" answer. This is the tension between "best" and "good." This Flexor might be a bigger challenge for you than you initially realize.

The Impacts at the Ends

If we need to be right and find the "best" answer, there are at least two big risks. Best thinking implies a world simple enough to make everything black or white. There is a best answer, and we need to find it . . .

When we have to *get it right*, we need to do enough analysis to confirm that we indeed have the right/best answer. A valuable endeavor, right? But there is a point beyond which the search for best leads us to paralysis by analysis. When we focus on the best answer, it becomes easier to judge other answers and opinions as wrong. In the worst case, we simply decide our preference is "right."

But we can lean too far into "good" too. Looking for a good answer implies there are other options worth considering. But going for good without defined criteria to measure it can lead us to the same place of judgment as leaning too far toward the "best" end of the spectrum. If we aren't careful, we allow *good* to be a subjective term—which can lead us into the same analysis trap as *best* can.

When to Apply It

The phrase "best practices" first came into vogue in the early 1900s as Frederick Taylor's approach to "scientific management" was the core of leadership thinking. When the system can be well defined and the variables largely understood and managed (i.e., the Clear context), best practices make sense. This was the context Taylor worked in, and so his approaches applied and were extremely helpful.

Since the 1990s, with the rise of quality management, process reengineering, and, later, Lean and Six Sigma, "best practices" came back into the spotlight. Again, the goal was to understand factors and find ways to reduce the variability until "best" could be found. When the context is Clear, best practices are still a worthy goal.

But when we find our context is Complicated or Complex, "best" gets in the way, and trying to force-fit the best practice will reduce engagement and cause frustration, poorer results, and unintended consequences. Sliding in the "good" direction on the spectrum allows us to consider various possibilities rather than seeking a perfect solution that may not exist.

I've often heard Dan Kennedy, a legendary business and marketing thought leader, say that "good is good enough." This phrase (as some of my team can attest) often resonates with me. He's saying that moving toward perfect might take longer than is needed. He is also implying that "perfect" isn't needed or perhaps even attainable. But as my team can also attest, this phrase can be frustrating (especially for people with a high natural inclination for valuing details). Leaning toward "good" rather than "best/right/perfect" is most helpful when the criteria and priorities are clear.

I remember sitting in a meeting as the coach of an executive. A few days later, he asked me what I thought about one of the presentations in the meeting. I said it seemed well thought out, very thorough, and well presented. Then I asked him why he asked. He said he couldn't figure out why so much time had been spent on it. Then he remembered asking one of the presenters an offhanded question a few weeks before: "I asked and thought I could get a back-of-the-envelope kind of answer—that is all I needed. Instead, I got three weeks' worth of effort in researching and recommendations." "Good" was all this leader wanted—but both because he was the boss and because he held people to high standards, they assumed (wouldn't you?) that he wanted the best possible answer. It was a big lesson for him, and a good example of this Flexor gone wrong.

How to Decide

Here are some ways to decide which direction to slide or lean on this Flexor.

Lean toward best when:
- the context is Clear, and most everything is known.
- best in this situation matters, not just to you but also to your team and the marketplace.
- a definitive best will lead to a competitive advantage.

Lean toward good when:

- there are unknowns and variables that are hard to control (i.e., Complicated and Complex contexts).
- you aren't sure there is enough information or time to get to the "best/right" answer.
- there are a variety (or at least a couple) of solutions you know will work or improve the situation.
- you recognize that the 80/20 rule is at play—that the marginal return of the effort to get to best might not add additional value.
- you can outline the criteria that can help you pick from your good options.
- the commitment and buy-in of those involved is more important than getting it perfect.
- you know you need to let go of your personal preference or need to be right (or someone helps you see that).

Here's a visual simplification:

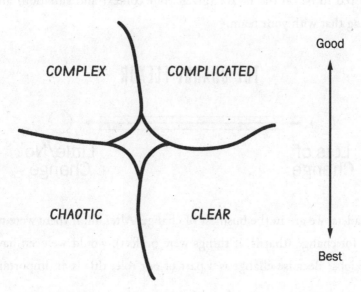

An Example

I will read this manuscript multiple times, as will others, including professional copy editors. And while we want to make sure we spell everything right and get all the commas in the right places, it is possible we will miss some. I know some have been missed in my other books, and I often see similar oversights in the books I read. A single "too" that should be a "two" isn't desirable. Fifteen of these mistakes are a problem. Fifteen isn't good enough, but is one okay? And how many iterations/edits would be required to get errors to zero? Is that time and effort worth it? These questions are the crux of the Best/Good Flexor.

For me, regarding this book, I am focused on "best" for word choice and examples, but I lean more toward "good" for grammar. Being clear on each of these factors for this Flexor helps me with my focus and priorities.

This example, as well as the example of my executive coaching client on page 86, highlights the importance of gaining clarity on where you need to be on the Flexor (given your context and situation) and sharing that with your team.

THE CHANGE FLEXOR

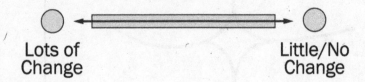

Lots of
Change

Little/No
Change

As leaders, we are in the business of change. After all, if there were no need for change (that is, if things were perfect), would we even have these jobs? Because change is a part of our role, this is an important

Flexor, yet one we often get wrong. When looking at a situation and thinking about this Flexor, the question isn't whether change is needed, but rather what rate/speed/amount of change is appropriate and how that will impact the acceptance of the changes you propose.

Rate of change must be considered in three dimensions:

- *Saturation*. Can people handle more change at this time? Consider your team (or individuals) as a glass and change as water. There is only so much water the glass can hold. Trying to put too much water in the glass will lead to a mess.

- *Readiness*. Do people think they can handle the change? Some people feel their glass is smaller, and sometimes people have other changes in their lives filling their glasses already. Are your people ready to handle more change at this moment? While people can use the "too much change!" argument as an excuse, there are real limits to our ability to process change.

- *Perception*. How do people view you when considering the rate of change? If you have ever had a new leader who walked in ready to make changes (immediately!) or one who left everything intact with no changes, you know what I'm talking about. How people perceive our intentions and the change itself has a big impact on how successful the change effort will be.

The Impacts at the Ends

Too much change too fast can be overwhelming and lead your team to question your motives. Is the change needed, or are you as the leader trying to make some sort of statement? We don't want to make change for change's sake, but you have heard the phrase and likely felt that way yourself. How successful were the changes when you heard/felt that sentiment?

Exactly.

Leaning too far into making change too fast can increase resistance, reduce change effectiveness, impact mental health, increase burnout, and more.

But . . .

If we don't change anything because we don't want to rock the boat, are overly worried about burnout, or want to make sure people are comfortable with us as a leader (in other words, leaning too far to the right on this Flexor), we are likely creating other problems.

When to Apply It

This is another Flexor that you will encounter regularly, because as we've said, as leaders we are in the business of change. The question it raises is: How much and how fast? It is closely linked to the Outcomes/ Others Flexor—because the more we might be leaning toward outcomes, the more we might also be leaning toward more rapid change.

I mean, if we need to reach these outcomes, we need to change some things . . .

Our Context Map is especially important to this Flexor. Let's look at the summary again and use it to help us decide where to be on the change spectrum.

UNORDERED **ORDERED**

COMPLEX

- There are unknown unknowns
- Competing ideas
  and opinions exist
- Things are unpredictable
  and unstable
- Paradox and contradictions exist
- Need for ideas and innovation

COMPLICATED

- There are knowns and unknowns
- We can forecast or guess
  but it is hard to definitely know
- Experts are needed
- Situational analysis needed

CHAOTIC

- There are unknowables!
- High turbulence and tension
- No patterns seem to exist
- No time to think
- Many decisions to make . . .
  now

CLEAR

- The knowns are known
- Familiar and known patterns
- Wide agreement on cause and effect
- We have the facts
  and they are indisputable
- Obvious and agreed-on solutions

How to Decide

There is art in this Flexor. It requires us to balance the real business need for changes with the readiness and perception of the team. Here are some ways to decide which direction to slide or lean on this Flexor.

Lean toward more change when:

- the context is Clear: people are more likely to see if there are issues or challenges.

- the context is Complicated, and you are seen as an expert, or you are getting expert intel from others (and that intel/experience makes a compelling case for the change).
- the context is Chaotic and people know that something needs to change.
- people feel somewhat settled and aren't feeling change saturation.
- there is a general feeling or unquestioned business needs that require change for improvement.

Lean toward little or no change when:
- the context is Complex. Slow down your rate of change to make sure you have all other voices and perspectives involved (either in the change itself or the change plan).
- there are lots of other changes going on. If you are a leader in the middle of the organization, you will be asked to lead/ champion changes, but you may have other intra-team or department changes that you might pause or delay if the total amount of change is high.
- trust is low. When people don't yet trust you or understand your intention, slowing down will likely increase your success.

As you can see, the Change Flexor isn't as simple as some others— there are many factors other than the specific context itself that play into how you might want to lean. That makes this visual simplification less simple.

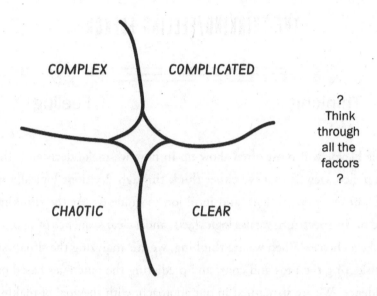

An Example

You've been planning to make some changes in your department. You have thought it through and gotten input from the team, and you seem to have buy-in from most people. Just when you are about to implement the change, something big happens in the organization: a merger, a sale, a new product launch, or anything that creates uncertainty or additional changes to your team. Then you must reassess the need and timing of your planned change. Use the Flexor to help you think about team readiness. Maybe the team will be ready to change something they have more control over. Maybe you can help them see that these changes will better position them for what might come next, even if it feels like a lot all at once. Thinking about these types of impacts will help you slide yourself on the Change Flexor scale to make a more informed timing decision.

THE THINKING/FEELING FLEXOR

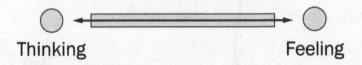

Thinking   Feeling

This Flexor will most often show up in how we make decisions. The simplified view is that we either think through decisions logically or use our emotions, values, and intuition to guide us. At the thinking end of the spectrum, we use logic, facts, and a clear sequence of steps to make a choice. When we are thinking, we are analyzing the situation, considering the pros and cons, and predicting the outcomes based on evidence. We are structured in our approach, with the goal of making the most rational and effective decision possible.

At the other end of the spectrum is feeling. This approach considers how a decision will affect us and everyone else involved. It prioritizes what feels right or what aligns with one's personal beliefs and desires. Decisions made this way are often based on gut instincts or emotional reactions, and they focus on maintaining harmony and personal satisfaction. From the thinking perspective, the feeling decision might not seem logical.

This dichotomy is one of the dimensions in the Myers-Briggs model. If you have taken this assessment, you have either a T or an F as a part of your style. While the model clearly recognizes this as a spectrum, the T or F has, for many familiar with their Myers-Briggs type, become a part of their identity.

The Impacts at the Ends

It is hard to argue logically against making logical decisions. And if you naturally or normally lean toward the feeling end of the Flexor, you know what I mean. When we anchor ourselves in the facts, logic, and data, they seem to be all that matters. But decisions made (individually or in a group) solely on the facts run the risk of being seen as tone deaf, uncaring, and shortsighted.

Consider the logical decision of Coca-Cola's introduction of New Coke in 1985. The decision was based on extensive market research and blind taste tests, which consistently showed that consumers preferred the sweeter taste of Pepsi, Coke's biggest rival. But the company underestimated the emotional attachment consumers had to the original Coke formula. The public reaction was overwhelmingly negative, with a strong emotional backlash against the change.

Compare that to the merger of AOL and Time Warner in 2000. The merger occurred during the height and hype of the dot-com boom and the excitement about the future of the internet. More time to evaluate the issues with the inevitable rapid technological change, the true value of AOL (for whom dial-up internet was its biggest revenue source), and massive gaps in the company cultures might have led to a different decision.

I know these are old examples, but you experience this Flexor nearly every day. If you lean too far toward thinking and logic, you might overlook team dynamics when building a project team. If you base your selections purely on experience or qualifications but ignore how people interact with each other or how they might view the selection, you might not get the results you want. And if you lean too far toward feelings, you might avoid a tough conversation because you don't want to hurt someone's feelings, even though there is a real problem that needs to be solved.

When to Apply It

I have included this as one of the Big Flexors because we likely have strong tendencies in the use of this Flexor, and it can be tied closely to our identity (for example, "I'm an engineer," or "I'm an accountant," so of course "I must value the facts above all else"). But this is an Everyday Flexor, too, because you make hundreds of small decisions every day, many automatically.

That is why "when to apply" this Flexor is multiple times each day. For many of the day-to-day decisions we all make, relying on our experience and tendency is fine. But as a leader, there are many decisions that might seem small to us but impact others more directly, so being more intentional about where we are on this Flexor can be helpful.

How to Decide

As a rule of thumb, the bigger the decision, and the more people who are involved, the more you need to consider where you are on this Flexor. Here are some specifics.

Lean toward thinking when:
- the context is Clear (truly Clear, not just assumed by you).
- things are Chaotic. In these cases, people will value any decision as helpful in the short term.
- people will agree with or follow your decision, regardless of what it is.
- there are mutually clear goals.

Lean toward feeling when:
- the context is Complicated, and you want and need the input of others—including their feelings.
- the context is Complex, with multiple competing ideas and opinions that exist.
- not all the facts are available.

- your intuition is telling you something different than where the facts as understood point you.
- you sense that team members have opinions (thoughts and feelings) that need to be heard.
- you have a bodily reaction that confirms or disputes the decision you are about to make.

Here's a visual simplification:

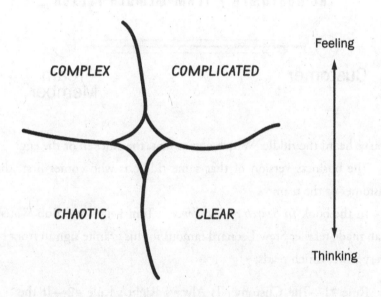

An Example

When you ask for someone's opinion or ideas, what do you ask them?

Do you ask . . .

"What do you think?"

Or . . .

"How do you feel?"

Whichever is your normal question probably says something about your natural tendency. If you want to be more effective in using this Flexor, ask people both questions. Make it safe for people to share their opinions and not just the facts. It will help you see a more complete picture of the situation and help you decide which direction to lean on this Flexor in that situation.

THE CUSTOMER / TEAM MEMBER FLEXOR

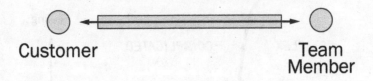

Customer   **Team Member**

You've heard the riddle: Which comes first, the chicken or the egg?

The business version of that same riddle is who comes first, the customer or the team?

In the book *In Search of Excellence*,[22] Tom Peters and Bob Waterman made retailer Stew Leonard famous for his granite sign in front of every store, which reads:

Rule #1—The Customer Is Always Right"; Rule #2—If the Customer Is Ever Wrong, Reread Rule #1

While you may not have shopped at one of Stew Leonard's regional dairy stores, chances are you have stayed at a Marriott property. Their first core value is:

Take care of associates and they will take care of the customers.[23]

Those two statements describe the ends of this Flexor, and, as with the riddle, you can make a case for either end.

When you view your customers and your team members as nodes in a network, more symbiotic than competitive, you have a chance to make this Flexor far more powerful in creating new results.

The Impacts at the Ends

I grew up in a family farm and agricultural service business and was drilled in the customer ethic. If the customer needed something, we did our best to meet their needs. My dad would have applauded Stew Leonard's sign in front of each store. But if the customer is always right, what if they mistreat, curse at, or abuse an employee? Will that impact employee mental health, company culture, and retention levels?

But what if you sit in the employee end of this spectrum as an organization? Will you "fire" customers without holding your team accountable for their role in customer service issues?

Questions like these are real challenges to think about beyond a riddle, and leaders need to give serious consideration to this Flexor.

When to Apply It

Stew Leonard and Marriott are successful, well-respected enterprises, and yet they start at very different places on this spectrum. Both have invested heavily for a very long time in building that "customer first" or "employee first" value into their cultures. If your organization has done that (beyond just listing some values on the website), then perhaps this Flexor won't be the most important one to you, as long as you're with that organization. However, if you experience ongoing challenges in a particular realm of the business, looking at alternatives on the opposite end of this Flexor (compared to your cultural norms) might provide a perspective to you and other leaders that would be helpful.

But philosophically, you need to know where you stand on this Flexor so that you can most effectively shift when needed. The questions on page 99 matter—and your answers will impact your customers, team, and organization.

How to Decide

Lean toward the customer when:

- it is Chaotic. The team might need to step up, because if the customers leave you, you have no business.
- the culture is strong. While you don't want abuse or to assume people won't leave, these may be times everyone can rally around a customer's need or situation.
- the team buys into the mission. When the team knows the why of the business (which involves the customer), we can lean in the direction of the customer.

Lean toward team members when:

- processes are strong and stable. If the processes are delivering for the customer, we can pay more attention to the needs of the team as a balance.
- the team is stressed or overwhelmed. When we take care of the team, as Marriott says, they will be better able to serve the customer.
- your people have been running hard. If the team has been going 110% on a project for weeks or months, you need to make sure you are taking care of their needs, even if the customer isn't thrilled (or asking for even more).

As you can see for this advice, this is another Flexor where the Context Map isn't our only guide. Factors like your organizational culture add another level of consideration beyond the context of the specific situation.

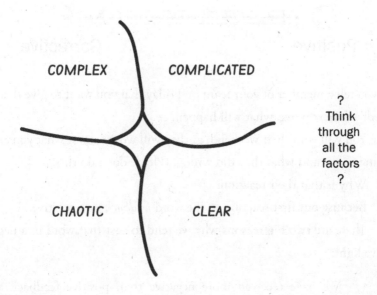

An Example

I've shared my starting point on this Flexor. It comes from my upbringing, my time as a salesperson, and my time as a business owner. I've thought and said, "We need to treat the customer like gold—after all, they write our paychecks!" But I've learned that sometimes "the customer is always right" is not so black and white. If the customer is hurting morale, causing unnecessary stress, or generally making it too hard for us, maybe they are the source of problems. Beyond strong company values, there are two sides to a story or situation, and team members and your customers often have different perspectives. It is our job to understand both in context so we can flex as needed.

Those moments of flex might be opportunities to deepen your relationships with both your customers and your team.

THE FEEDBACK FLEXOR

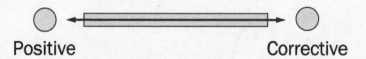

Positive   Corrective

If you tell a member of your team on Friday that you want to give them feedback next week, what will happen?

You will ruin their weekend, as they will worry about what you are going to say and what they did wrong. (Please don't do this!)

Why is that their reaction?

Because our first reaction to the word *feedback* isn't positive.

There are two big reasons why we tend to cast that word in a negative light:

- We have received more negative than positive feedback at work.
- We remember the negative longer than the positive. This is a simple description of the negativity bias, and it is real.

You may not feel the need for positive feedback yourself ("I succeeded without it; so can others."). But I submit that you would have succeeded faster and been even more effective if you had received appropriate, specific, and timely positive feedback.

The Feedback Flexor challenges us to consider the role of both positive and negative feedback in helping others grow and succeed.

The Impacts at the Ends

On one extreme is the "praise is powerful" crowd. Tell people they are doing great, keep the energy up, and make people more confident with positive feedback. The downsides of this approach include:

- *Complacency.* People may stop improving because they are apparently doing great already.
- *Ego.* While a healthy ego is important, if our ego gets too big—well, we know there are problems with that.
- *Dependency.* Positive feedback can be like too much of any good thing. We want more of it, in this case for validation.
- *Minimizing areas of improvement.* If the areas for improvement are ignored or overshadowed by the positive, they may never be addressed.

In workshops over the last 30 years, I have heard all these cases against positive feedback hundreds of times. While all of these are real risks, there are risks at the other end of the spectrum too.

If all the feedback is negative, you may find:

- *Lower morale.* Constant criticism can demoralize both individuals and the team.
- *Reduced trust.* If the feedback is viewed as overly harsh or unnecessary, relationships and communication can be negatively impacted.
- *Negative culture.* If all feedback from you is negative, others will tend to share the same with each other. Chances are that isn't the culture you desire.
- *Increased turnover.* Ongoing negative feedback can lead to dissatisfaction, leaving people to look for a different working environment.

It's pretty clear that neither of these sets of outcomes is what we want—and if we are experiencing them, we aren't likely looking at ourselves (enough). That is the power of this Flexor.

Let me be clear—this Flexor doesn't suggest we make things up, spin things, sugarcoat, or make light of problems. Effective feedback, positive or negative, needs to be specific with examples, meaningful, clear, kind, and timely. These criteria apply equally to both positive and negative feedback.

When to Apply It

While there isn't concrete and reliable evidence of the ideal ratio of positive to negative (praise to criticism), the basic premise is that both are needed, and most likely more positive than negative (everything else being equal). Once we see the general value of feedback being more balanced, we must realize that the balance develops over time, not in every conversation or situation.

And that is pretty simple. If something needs to be corrected, help people correct it (and you may not need any positive feedback in that conversation). If something went well, specifically share what you saw that was awesome, and don't wait for a negative to go with it.

How to Decide

While you probably have this one down in practice, just to be clear:

Lean toward corrective when:
- people are doing something unsafe or unethical or are unaware of the possible consequences.
- something needs to be corrected before it becomes a new (bad) habit.

- there are significantly better ways to do something.
- you want to help people improve their performance, behaviors, or results.

Lean toward positive when:
- people don't know they are doing something well.
- you want to reinforce positive behaviors.
- you want to recognize people doing things that are valuable to the larger team or others.
- you want to encourage and build confidence in the team's performance, behaviors, or results.

This important coaching Flexor is unique in that it relies on the context of performance, behavior, or results and is interconnected with other Flexors (like the Thinking/Feeling and Truth/Grace Flexors, for example). This is why you don't see advice next to the Context Map below. Use these other factors and this image as your guide when considering this Flexor.

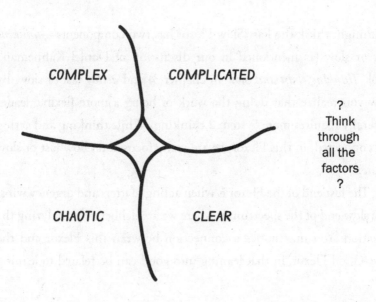

An Example

In many work situations, people are doing some things well and can improve on others. It is our job to help them see and understand the implications of both! If I watched you give a presentation yesterday, I likely saw some things you did well and some other areas where you could improve. At some point, I need to share both. When and how I share each (how I lean on this Flexor in the moment) may depend on your emotional state, confidence, and other factors. You will be in the best position to continue to grow and improve when you understand all those things.

THE FAST/SLOW FLEXOR

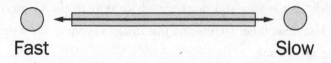

Fast   Slow

You might think the Fast/Slow Flexor has two components—*thinking* fast or slow (as mentioned in our discussion of Daniel Kahneman's book *Thinking, Fast and Slow* in chapter 3) and *acting* fast or slow. By now you realize that doing the work of being a more flexible leader generally requires more System 2 thinking. While thinking and acting are connected, in this Flexor we are really focused on how fast or slow we *act*.

The fast end of the Flexor is when acting matters and urgency wins. The slow end of the spectrum is where we are deliberately analyzing the situation. You may notice a connection between this Flexor and the Best/Good Flexor, in that leaning into good can be related to leaning into slow. If these are both your tendencies, pay close attention to these two Flexors.

The Impacts at the Ends

Speed.

Whether we want speed to market, to go "full speed ahead," to feel the need for speed, to accelerate successful execution, or to use speed as a competitive tool, speed seems to be everywhere. (By the way, all five of these phrases come directly from the titles of business books written in the last decade.)

We see speed as a descriptor of our world, and, for many, a definer of our lives.

And while speed is important, at the far left of this Flexor, speed—as on the highway—can also kill.

Take Boeing and its desire to release the 737 MAX aircraft.

In their haste to bring this plane to market (and compete with Airbus's A320neo), Boeing implemented a new software feature called the Maneuvering Characteristics Augmentation System (MCAS), designed to improve aircraft handling and prevent stalling. The MCAS software relied on just one sensor, with no redundancies built in. That, along with inadequate pilot training, contributed to two fatal crashes: Lion Air Flight 610 in October 2018 and Ethiopian Airlines Flight 302 in March 2019. These tragedies resulted in the deaths of 346 people and led to a global grounding of all 737 MAX aircraft. Beyond the loss of life, the need for speed to market also led to significant financial losses, damage to company reputation, and numerous lawsuits and investigations.

Going too slow has risks too. I don't even need to tell the stories for you to recognize how being overly slow caused problems (and an ultimate demise) for BlackBerry, Kodak, and Blockbuster. Slowing down to try to minimize risk can be a risk itself. Analysis paralysis is more than just a clever turn of a phrase—it can keep us from succeeding or even surviving.

When to Apply It

While true with all the Flexors, in the Fast/Slow Flexor I believe you must look outside yourself for input—and heed what you hear. Models like DISC measure our natural pace, and due to that natural tendency we might justify our place on this Flexor too quickly. In workshops, I have asked people, based on this Flexor, to describe how long it took for them to decide to purchase a new vehicle. During the debrief, I have received answers ranging from one hour to two years. While those answers might work for an individual, when leading a team where the stakes of the decision might be bigger, neither of those answers at the extreme end of this flexor are likely best.

For decisions of any magnitude and/or that impact the lives and work of more people, ask yourself this question: How important is speed to the making of this decision? For the "fast crowd," even asking the question slows us down a bit.

While my natural pace is left of center on this Flexor, I have learned the value of leaning to the right. It is my experience that external factors push many leaders toward the left even if it isn't our natural tendency.

Everything else being equal, because so many external drivers lean toward speed, I often encourage leaders to slide to the slower side of this Flexor.

How to Decide

Lean toward fast when:
- the context is Clear. When the data is there, the process is outlined and clear, and everyone agrees, speed will be helpful.
- the context is Chaotic. When everything is uncertain, speed of decision and action helps settle things down. Now you and your team have something to work from and react to, as opposed to being immobilized by uncertainty.

Lean toward slow when:
- the context is Complicated. When we know we don't know things, we should slow down to get the insights and opinions of others, especially those with expertise. Time spent here will be valuable in terms of the decision itself and its acceptance.
- the context is Complex. If things are unpredictable and unstable, you need ideas and to try new things. Pilots or tests, rather than full-blown decisions, will likely be most effective here.
- you have time or can make time. Sometimes urgency is implied but not needed. The phrase "go slow to go fast" contains much wisdom.
- speed isn't the first criteria. Often, problems or questions come to us as leaders and we assume people want a response right away—or we feel that we will show we care by responding quickly. Ask how important speed is before assuming the need is critical/urgent.

Here's a visual simplification:

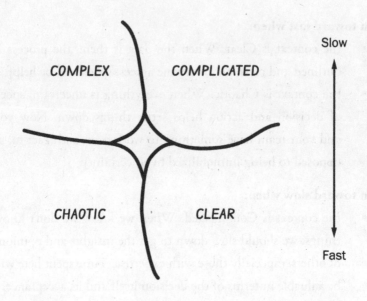

An Example

Here are two simple and relatively common examples.

Someone comes to your office with a question or sends you an email on Friday afternoon. Do you need to rush to a decision, or can you sleep on it and wait until Monday? While there is an advantage to crossing it off your list and looking responsive and on the ball, is that more important than having a better answer or solution?

Or . . .

Have you ever put off or procrastinated on something because you perceived that the conversation would be hard or unpleasant, even though you already knew your decision?

In both situations, using the Fast/Slow Flexor will help you decide your best course of action.

THE STRENGTH/WARMTH FLEXOR

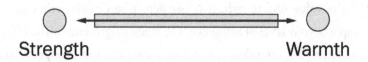

One way to look at how we influence others is to consider strength and warmth. We can find examples of well-known leaders who tend to lead at each end of this spectrum. On the strength end, we can look at leaders like:

- Steve Jobs
- Margaret Thatcher
- Elon Musk
- Donald Trump

Each is influential to those who view their strength, competence, confidence, and assurance as reasons why they are fit to lead.

On the other end of the spectrum, we might consider these people as highly influential because of their warm characteristics:

- Martin Luther King Jr.
- Oprah Winfrey
- Jimmy Carter

These influential people would be more likely described as caring, empathetic, and trusting—characteristics of warmth.

While many people believe (and try to lead by the belief) that strength, power, and position are the most influential factors, research in behavioral science says that both factors—strength and warmth—are useful. In fact, much of that research says that if you had to lean to one side, warmth might be your better choice.

The Impacts at the Ends

For all the value of strength, it is the perception of the other person that impacts your level of influence. On the strength end of the Flexor, we have aptitudes, confidence, experiences, action. But those attributes (especially without clear intention) can be seen as overconfidence and being showy, too dominant, and overly focused on position and compliance. On the warmth end, great traits like empathy, caring, affection, and trust can be seen as being touchy-feely, overly emotional, a pushover, or indecisive.

Like all the other Flexors, you can clearly see the problems in over-relying on either end.

When to Apply It

You will want to consider this Flexor whenever you want to influence, which as a leader is all the time. The best way to gain influence is to combine strength and warmth, and to specifically lead with warmth early in the relationship. When people see us as warm, trust is built faster, and communication becomes more effective sooner. Prioritizing warmth also impacts empathy and understanding.

How to Decide

Lean toward strength when:
- the context is Clear. When the facts exist and people understand them, your strength, confidence, and decisiveness can be very helpful.

- the context is Chaotic. When there is much tension and there is no time to think, people are looking for someone to lead. When you lead from strength in these moments, you will become even more influential.
- trust is already high. When people understand your intention and know you have their best interests in mind, others will see your strength as a positive attribute.
- you are working with people who personally value strength more.

Lean toward warmth when:
- it is early in your relationship with others.
- the context is Complicated. In these cases, when you need others and their input, your openness to them and their thoughts will pay off in both the information you gather and the relationships you build.
- the context is Complex. Here you need input, and you need people to feel safe to share their opinions, which might not be popular. Showing warmth will serve you well in these situations.
- you are working with people who personally value warmth more.

Here's a visual simplification:

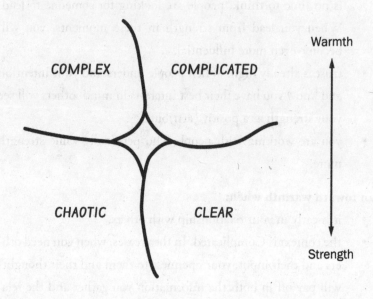

An Example

You are trying to influence a group of stakeholders to support the project your team is proposing. You want to appear confident and strong, but you don't have positional power or know all the players in the room personally. Leaning into warmth is probably a better place to start. Focus on building relationships and communicating even before the meeting begins. Because you opened by listening to them and valuing who they are, they will likely be more open to hearing the details and specifics of your plan.

THE TRUTH/GRACE FLEXOR

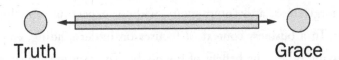

Truth   Grace

Based on your background or beliefs, this Flexor might give you pause. What is truth, and more specifically, what is grace? Grace has a very specific meaning to me as a follower of Jesus. I believe Jesus was the exemplar for all of us in having both truth and grace, and we can learn much from His example.

And . . .

I know that statement might concern you and that the word *grace* might be getting in your way.

But I don't want it to.

Acknowledging that, please read on, because I'm guessing the leaders you most admire, regardless of your (or their) spiritual backgrounds or beliefs, have done a good (or even excellent) job balancing this Flexor. You can think of this Flexor in communication, relationships, decision-making, or coaching.

Let's define both truth and grace in a secular way.

At the truth end of the Flexor, we are focused on the quality or state of being true. We want to be honest and accurate and to present facts and viewpoints without distortion. Typically, the focus is on clarity, correctness, and, sometimes, blunt honesty. It is concerned with what is right, factual, "telling it like it is."

In decision-making, coaching, and communication, a focus on truth prioritizes clarity, accuracy, and directness. This can be especially important when facts and accuracies are necessary for safety, justice, or legal reasons.

And then there is the grace end of the Flexor. A grace focus leans toward creating goodwill. It is more than politeness, but includes kindness, forgiveness, and compassion—without expecting something in return. In a business context, it focuses on understanding, empathy, and giving others the benefit of the doubt. To grant grace also means being patient, even if that patience doesn't seem warranted and might not be reciprocated. Patience, in some situations, can be challenging for me. But I have learned over and over that when I intentionally flex toward grace, good things result.

In the workplace, a focus on grace means holding a positive intent for others and expecting positive outcomes. It might also involve overlooking minor mistakes, offering unsolicited kindness, or supporting others even if those actions might be uncomfortable or unpopular.

The Impacts at the Ends

Truth is truth. There are facts, data, and results—and they can't be denied. Sometimes they are good and sometimes they aren't. But chances are you have experienced someone offering those facts in a tell-it-like-it-is approach and being less than successful. When the news or facts aren't good, a focus on truth without grace (even for those who say to "just tell me") can create defensiveness and reduce trust. Even when the facts are positive, a complete focus on truth might lead to an incomplete view of the situation and leave people wondering why there isn't any celebration or acknowledgment of the successful outcomes.

A complete focus on grace can obscure or bend the facts or leave people with a false sense of the truth. Being too worried about how people will feel about the truth may lead to reduced expectations, a false sense of performance, or even complacency.

As with all the Flexors, both ends are valuable, but are far less valuable when taken individually without the accompanying factor as a balance.

When to Apply It

Stop and consider the truth/grace balance when you are communicating messages that might seem tough or hard for others to receive, when there are high emotions around a change or decision, or any time you sense that more empathy might be helpful.

Since grace may take time, when you feel a strong sense of urgency to communicate, decide, or coach, that might be a time you remind yourself to consider this Flexor before you act.

How to Decide

Lean toward truth when:
- the context is Clear. Facts here are generally mutually understood and so are more likely to be accepted.
- the context is Chaotic. And the uncertainty level is so high that people need something to hang on to. While in these situations truth might be hard to find, people will accept the direction and assurance truth can provide.
- there is a level of calmness. Emotions—both yours and those of others—are managed enough that the truth can be heard.

Lean toward grace when:
- the context is Complicated or Complex and the unknowns are causing anxiety, fear, or uncertainty.

- emotions are high. The truth needs to be shared, but maybe not at this moment. Waiting in this case is an example of grace—for both you and the other person.
- the other people or person seem closed off. More truth when people are defensive likely won't work. Support and empathy, examples of grace in action, can be an antidote to defensiveness.
- people are misunderstanding you. When our intentions are benevolent but misunderstood, we can get indignant and want to prove ourselves. This rarely helps. Granting grace, however, has a better chance.

Here's a visual simplification:

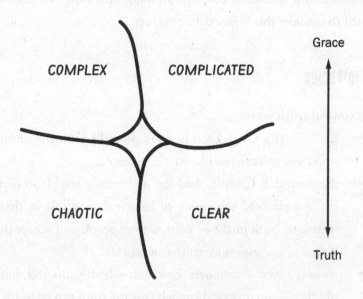

An Example

Consider if a member of your team makes a grave error in their work. The error needs to be corrected and can't be overlooked. In this case, the truth must be shared in a direct and honest way. But it can still be delivered with kindness and consideration. Offering grace doesn't mean spinning or lessening the message; it means sharing the message in a way that is both clear and kind (and far more likely to be heard and accepted).

STEPPING BACK

These Big Picture Flexors cover a lot of ground, and when we use them intentionally, they can help us lead more situationally and successfully. Spend time thinking about and applying these Flexors right away. The following questions can help you get started.

PAUSE AND REFLECT

Before you move on, take a minute to think about these questions. (Even better if you take some notes on your thoughts!)

- Which of these Flexors caused me to pause or created the biggest aha moment for me?
- Which do I think I am best at flexing on now?
- Which Flexor do I think I am poorest at, or do I feel most concerned about?
- How could I get some feedback from my team on my ability to flex in these ways?

RESOURCES TO HELP YOU LEAD FLEXIBLY

You can get a pocket guide to all the Flexors at FlexibleLeadershipBook. com or by scanning this QR code.

> The core idea is that there is almost always a range of approaches you can take on a spectrum of options, and that the best choice won't always be the same in every situation or our personal favorite. Finding the right course of action requires you to choose based on the situational needs you face.

CHAPTER 9

THE EVERYDAY FLEXORS

> An effective leader allows exceptions to the rule for exceptional results or when circumstance demands.
> —John Wooden, Hall of Fame basketball coach[24]

Now that we have explored the Big Picture Flexors, let's look at those I call the Everyday Flexors. Just like those we have already talked about, they challenge us to flex our approach based on the situation. The difference is that these may be Flexors that you experience more frequently.

While the Big Picture Flexors are practical, with these you will have the chance to use/practice them quite literally every day. You will also see that as you get more proficient and comfortable with the Big Picture Flexors, these will get easier to use. And remember, just like the Big Picture Flexors, finding the right course of action requires you to choose based on the situational needs you face.

We'll outline these Everyday Flexors as we did in the previous chapter. For each, we'll explore:

- the nature of the Flexor
- the impacts at the ends of the spectrum
- when to apply it
- how to decide
- an example to make it more tangible

As you read each of them, remember that the art of Flexible Leadership is remembering that success is rarely at the extreme ends of the Flexor spectrum but will often lie somewhere between those extremes. Your intention and the context of the situation will help you find where to land within the center band.

THE TASK/PEOPLE FLEXOR

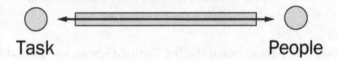

Task   People

The Task/People Flexor is closely related to the Outcomes/Others Flexor but is more immediate and direct, and somewhat less philosophical. This is an everyday, real-life Flexor. Nearly everything we do as leaders is influenced by this question: *Which is my priority, the work (task) or the people doing the work?*

Common and well-established communication and style tools like DISC (in its many forms) and Myers-Briggs measure our tendencies on this spectrum. But as we've talked about throughout this book, while it is helpful to know and understand our style and preferences, that is only a starting point in us leading others successfully.

Before we explore this Flexor, let's be clear. Regardless of your preferences or natural inclinations, if you have a strong lean toward tasks, you will still care about people, and if you lean strongly toward people, you will still get work done. But your choices, conscious or not, on this Flexor have big implications for your success in getting things done with others.

The Impacts at the Ends

Consider the metaphorical bull in the china shop. If the bull is just trying to get through the shop to reach something to eat across the store, it will get there. But oh, the carnage left in its wake! You may know a person like that. In their zeal, passion, and focus to get things accomplished (all good things), they don't seem too worried about what or who is impacted—the task is their focus and their goal.

It is admirable to get the task accomplished, but to what ends?

On the opposite end of the spectrum, complete focus is directly on the people and their needs. This seems great—unless the work isn't getting done!

Like all the Flexors, there is merit and value at each end, but the biggest unintended consequences occur when living at the ends too.

When to Apply It

You can apply this Flexor to nearly any task you have, conversation you hold, email you send, and meeting you attend or facilitate. Ask yourself: *Which is more important right now, the completion of the task or the needs and opinions of the people?* Your answer will guide you on this Flexor and will likely impact where you will land on the Compliance/Commitment Flexor too.

How to Decide

Lean toward task when:

- the context is Clear. As clarity across the team grows, the more you can lean in the direction of the task itself.

- the context is Chaotic. The uncertainty of the situation leads everyone to have something to hold on to. While you need to recognize that people need help, the help they most need is some direction.

- people ask for direction. If people are looking for you to provide them direction, give it to them.

- the expectations are mutually clear. When you know that people know what is expected, their level of confidence will be higher, you can lean into the specifics of the task, and keep the task top of mind.

Lean toward people when:

- the context is Complicated. As we have said, uncertainty is hard for us to deal with. This is the time to check with people about how they are feeling and what their thoughts about the situation, decision, or change looks like.

- the context is Complex. When you can't capture or know all the relevant facts, you need people's insights and opinions. Creating the dialogue about the situation is a "people lean" but helps you move the task forward too.

- you sense tension, unrest, confusion, or anxiety. When you sense any emotion with an individual or the team, consider that a flag to both slow down (the Fast/Slow Flexor) and check in with people.

- you can't tell where people stand. If you can't tell, chances are you are missing something. Just because they don't look tense or aren't expressing concerns doesn't mean they don't have them. When you aren't sure, take your foot off the task accelerator and be more empathetic.

Here's a visual simplification:

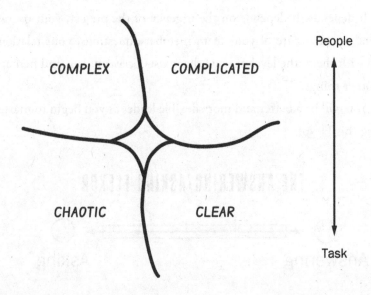

An Example

Imagine there is a project you need to finish and have scheduled some time to work on it at 2 PM today. The task is important, and you want to make sure you get it done. If you have a task focus, you will do everything you can to start at 2 PM. If a person comes to you with a question at 1:55, you may want to help them, but your mind will keep pointing you to the project. You might even help the person, but they might (even without you being aware) feel you are rushing them or are not fully present with them.

If the situation is the same, but you take a more people focus, you will likely worry less about the project when the person comes to you with their question at 1:55. You might be more present with them, even if you know it might impact your project timeline a bit.

Which is the right answer?

It depends. It depends on the urgency of the project, your overall calendar, the nature of your team member's questions, your relationship with them, the level of trust that exists between you, and perhaps 50 other things.

You will be a better and more flexible leader as you begin to master using this Flexor.

THE ANSWERING/ASKING FLEXOR

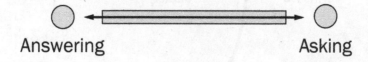

Answering   Asking

As a leader, you likely feel like you are supposed to have answers. After all, you were promoted because of your skill and knowledge, right? While it sometimes feels like a weight, you feel you are supposed to have answers for the questions you face.

On the other hand, have you ever had a boss who seemed to know it all? While we all want knowledgeable and competent bosses, are those who act like they know everything among the most effective leaders you have had?

Based on informally asking hundreds of people that question, my guess is you are shaking your head no.

When someone asks you a question, you have two possible responses: to answer the question or to ask another question back in response. Which you choose and how often you make that choice reveals your starting point on the Answering/Asking Flexor.

The Impacts at the Ends

While everyone wants a leader who is competent and knowledgeable, and it is easy to ask a question and get an answer, we also want our opinions and ideas to be heard. When you are focused on having the answers (either because you believe you do or think you are supposed to), you squelch the ideas of others and reduce people's confidence in their own answers. Beyond that, always being on the answering end likely leads you to the compliance end of the Compliance/Commitment Flexor too.

When people ask you questions and you always provide definite answers, soon they may stop thinking for themselves—or feel that you don't want them to. And all you might get is, "Whatever you say, Boss."

But if you lean too far toward asking, people might feel you don't know anything or won't give them a straight answer. If someone always answers your question with another question, your trust in them might wane, and your frustration might grow. While always having an answer isn't always helpful, never having one is a problem too.

When to Apply It

Since we are asked questions all day long, in meetings, instant messages, on phone calls, in emails, and in conversations both in person and virtually, you have plenty of chances to practice this one.

How to Decide

Lean toward answering when:

- the context is Clear. In these cases, there is likely a clear, unassailable answer, and you know it.
- it will be much faster to just answer. Yes, you could send them to the intranet or ask a teammate. But unless you want to teach them to use those resources, just giving the answer is likely the most practical and effective method.
- the need is urgent. Related to the last point, think about the Fast/Slow Flexor. If you have the answer, you providing it is the faster option.
- you don't want to consider other options. There is no reason for you to ask if you already have the facts or a decision.

Lean toward asking when:

- the context is Complicated or Complex. In these cases, their input is needed, especially if they have significant experience or a different perspective.
- you want to build their confidence.
- you want their input. If you are brainstorming or wanting their input, the sooner you provide your perspective, the less likely they will share theirs.
- there are multiple possible answers. Think about the Best/ Good Flexor—your right answer might not be the only good or possible answer.

Here's a visual simplification:

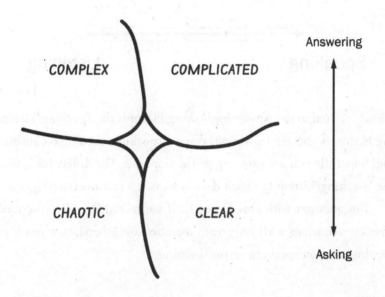

An Example

I could give you any number of examples here, but you will find five in the next two hours of work. Move on this Flexor based on your goals in the specific situation and with the specific person or group. If you want people to build their judgment and discernment skills, you need to ask them more often for their opinion and perspective. Generally speaking, if you want to lean toward commitment, you will likely also want to lean more toward asking.

A general rule of thumb to help you with this Flexor is to *ask more and assert less.*

But if you already know the answer or have already decided what course of action you are going to take, move toward answering. Few things feel like a "gotcha" moment and reduce trust more than asking for people's opinion when you don't care or it doesn't matter.

THE SPEAKING/LISTENING FLEXOR

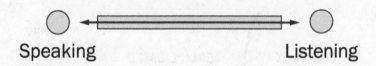

Closely related to the Answering/Asking Flexor is the Speaking/Listening Flexor. If you are answering, you are speaking. And if you are asking, hopefully you are listening to the response. The difference is that the Speaking/Listening Flexor doesn't require a question to trigger it.

The question with this Flexor is, if we recorded and transcribed your conversations with your team members (or others), how much of the time are you speaking versus listening?

The Impacts at the Ends

You've been in a meeting where someone dominates the conversation. They seem to go on and on—either repeating things they have already said, giving more, unneeded examples, or telling endless stories about the points they are trying to make. They speak so much that no one else has a chance to get their ideas and comments into the conversation. Often, it isn't a conversation at all. This person could be a leader or not; I'm sure you recognize this behavior.

I've asked hundreds of people over the years in workshops to describe challenging behaviors in meetings—those that keep meetings from being more effective. "The Dominator" is usually among the first things mentioned. Their behavior negatively impacts meetings, reduces engagement, and reduces trust between them and others.

Have you ever considered that the Dominator might be you?

At the same time, consider a leader at the other end of this spectrum. While listening is valuable, the team wants to hear from you as the leader. They want to know your perspective, insights, vision, and plans. If you always listen and never speak, trust will diminish, and uncertainty about you and your plans will grow.

When to Apply It

We can apply this Flexor at any moment when we are with others—because we are either talking or we aren't. While there is no guarantee we are listening just because we aren't speaking, we certainly can't be listening if we are speaking. A helpful acronym can help us use this Flexor where we are speaking. It is an especially helpful acronym because the word itself helps us be more intentional about what we do next.

The acronym is *WAIT.*

It stands for *Why Am I Talking?*

We can ask this question before we begin speaking or while we are speaking. If we don't have a good and valuable answer for why we are talking, we should probably stop. And once we stop, we can choose to listen.

Here are some related questions you could ask along with *Why Am I Talking?* All of these will help you with the Speaking/Listening Flexor:

- What am I gaining by speaking now?
- Has my point already been made?
- Is speaking helping me influence the other person?
- Is speaking helping to build my relationship or trust with the other person?

- What might be lost if I say too much?
- What might be gained if I say nothing or less?
- Am I impeding the other person from making their point?
- Am I helping the other person build their confidence?

All of these are valuable questions and apply to us in any human interaction. But when we consider them as a leader, the implications can be even more important. Why?

Because with the positional power that comes with our role, people are more likely to acquiesce to let us speak, even if it isn't in anyone's best interest. And it is more likely that the Speaking/Listening Flexor can remain a blind spot for us.

How to Decide

Lean toward speaking when:
- the context is Clear. When everyone has a level of agreement, your input as the leader will be valuable and confirming.
- the context is Chaotic. People are waiting for (and need) your input, guidance, and direction.
- you have something relevant to say.
- you have a point to make that hasn't yet been mentioned.
- people are asking for your opinion.

Lean toward listening when:
- the context is Complicated or Complex. In these situations, if you talk too much or too soon, you may keep others from sharing their perspectives, ideas, and opinions.
- you notice you are talking. Likely, if you've noticed, you've already been talking too long.

- you want the input of others. As the leader, the longer you talk, the less likely others will have anything to add. And don't just stop talking—actually listen to what others are communicating!

Here's a visual simplification:

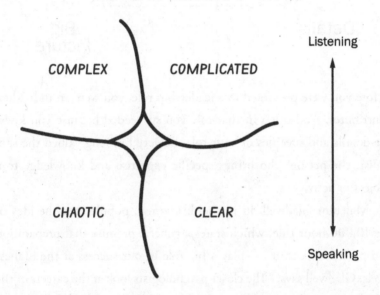

An Example

If you have feedback to give to a member of your team or someone else you are coaching, you are likely prepared with a list of the things you want to say. Remember, though, that the longer you talk, the less likely the other person will say anything. A great way to find a better balance on this Flexor is to ask them to *share their ideas first*. Once you listen to their points, giving yours will be easier (some will have already been discussed), and they will be far more likely to be accepted.

In general, remember to *talk less and talk later*. You will get more interaction as a leader when you let others speak first.

THE DETAILS / BIG PICTURE FLEXOR

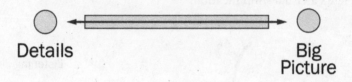

Details   Big
                          Picture

Before you were promoted to a leadership role, you were an individual contributor. And often in that role you succeeded because you knew the details and specifics of your role. Society has long valued the specialist: the person who brings specific expertise and knowledge to a subject or activity.

Malcolm Gladwell, in his book *Outliers*, popularized the idea of the 10,000-hour rule, which states a general premise that preparation and practice—lots of it—play a big role in our success at the highest levels. Gladwell says, "The closer psychologists look at the careers of the gifted, the smaller the role innate talent seems to play and the bigger the role preparation seems to play."[25]

The details clearly matter.

But there is something (big) to be said for a different perspective, a higher-level viewpoint too. In David Epstein's book *Range: Why Generalists Triumph in a Specialized World*,[26] he suggests that while specialization (majoring in the details) is valued by society, those who engage in a wide variety of experiences and skills (generalists) often solve more complex problems. Generalists are often better able to integrate diverse pieces of knowledge creatively and make novel connections, meaning they are effective in rapidly changing situations.

That sounds like leadership to me.

This Flexor is important both philosophically and practically, in part because many of us were selected as leaders because we were good at the details. But if we stay too long in the details, we may miss the big picture or find ourselves unable to see situations from new perspectives.

The Impacts at the Ends

A leader who needs to know all the details can probably still do the job they used to do and perhaps even relishes their expertise in those details. But if you work for that leader, you might feel you have no room for freedom, no chance to learn and grow, and you may feel micromanaged.

Another leader might always be thinking about the big picture. They have plenty of ideas, but they don't always seem so practical. Some of their insights may be of great value in the long term, perhaps even brilliant. But day to day, if you work for them, you might feel underappreciated and unsupported. It may seem like they either don't know much about your work or don't care about the details.

When to Apply It

While this isn't the tendency of every leader, you may have noted a general rule already—most leaders struggle with the left end of this spectrum (the details) more than leaning too far toward the big picture.

I often use the analogy of a forest to make this point. If you are a worm (not that I am suggesting you or any person is actually a worm) and you look at the tree in front of you, it will look like your whole world. It will define your perspective, describe your challenges, and impede your progress. Living too much in the "worm's-eye" view can do this to us.

But if you look at the same forest with a bird's-eye view, you see that same tree in a very different way. The tree is a part of a system, and the options for getting around seem obvious and almost endless. The bird's-eye view is necessary for us as leaders. We must be able to lift our eyes and see things our teams may not see. Only when we see our situation from this different vista can we help our teams see it too.

But the worm never sees it.

How to Decide

Lean toward details when:

- the context is Clear. The patterns we see in the details and specifics are helpful here, whether we see them as a leader or others share them with us. If we aren't in the details, we need to make sure others are.
- the context is Chaotic. We can't wax philosophical; we need to decide on a course of action—now. Details will be needed to do that.
- you have the requisite knowledge. When you know the details as the leader, you might be able to help. Warning—the longer it has been since you did the actual work in question, the less likely you know the details as well as you think. The world is changing, after all.

Lean toward big picture when:

- the context is Complicated or Complex. When there are unknowables, trying to lean into details will get you in trouble. You've heard of the danger of making assumptions—this is when it is especially dangerous.

- the team is missing this perspective. If you don't see the big picture, likely no one will. This is part of your job. Make sure you are lifting your eyes to see the landscape and the options it helps you see.
- the team is in conflict over the details. If you stay in the detail perspective with everyone else, you may be sucked into the conflict! But when you can help people see the bigger picture and understand the why and purpose of the work, conflicts about the details are more likely resolved.

Here's a visual simplification:

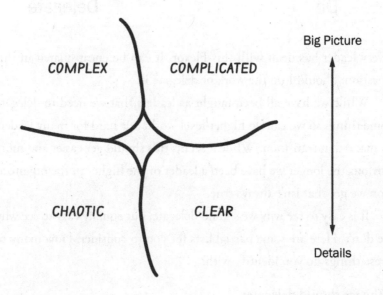

An Example

When forming a project team, you need a good balance on this Flexor. People need the big picture (e.g., Why are we here? What is the goal of this project?), and you need the details of the deliverables, stakeholders, roles, and expectations. If you are missing either of these perspectives, your project will flounder. As the project moves forward, the situation and dynamics might dictate that you move toward details to iron out a specific deliverable, for example. Or you might need to help people avoid scope creep by seeing the big picture and the value of continuing to make progress toward your important outcomes.

THE DO/DELEGATE FLEXOR

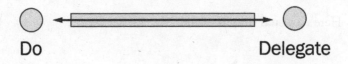

Do   Delegate

Every leader has dealt with this Flexor. It can be encapsulated in this question: Should I do the work or delegate it?

While we have all been taught as leaders that we need to delegate some things so we can do higher-level work, it is hard for many leaders to make that transition. While it seems this should get easier and more obvious the longer we have been a leader or the higher in the organization we go, that isn't always true.

It is easy to see why we should delegate, but equally easy to see why we don't. Here are some partial lists for you to consider. How many of these things do you identify with?

Why we should delegate:
- To develop others
- To create greater organizational capacity (when we delegate something, now two people can do it)
- To empower others

- To free our time to do other work (hopefully higher-value work we can't delegate)
- To reduce the perception of micromanagement

Why we don't delegate (i.e., reasons we do rather than delegate):
- We do work we are comfortable with.
- We do work we know.
- We do work we are good at.
- We do work that we have been recognized for.
- We do things that are tangible and measurable (and some of the leadership tasks we must do aren't so concrete).
- We do things because we can do them better than others.
- We do things because it would take us longer to teach them than just do them.

Looking at these lists, you can see why this Flexor is challenging for so many leaders.

The Impacts at the Ends

If you continue to do the work and never delegate, you will be completely overwhelmed, probably avoid some important but not urgent work, and be more likely to burn out. You also won't develop your team members and will have a hard time building the trust of your team. I could give you a longer list, but any one of these is reason enough to avoid the far-left end of this Flexor.

But if you delegate everything, you will likely have a significant perception and trust issue with your team too. They will wonder if you are in touch with the team, know anything or care at all about the work, and question your commitment. They will likely also want to know what you are doing with your time!

When to Apply It

As with the rest of the Flexors, the right answer is somewhere in the middle. You can consider where you are on this Flexor almost any day on any task. There are typically two perspectives to be aware of: your personal perspective, and the perspective of your team. Here are two common situations as examples:

- When your to-do list looks exceptionally long, ask yourself: Am I delegating enough?
- When people are looking for growth opportunities, ask yourself: Am I delegating enough?

How to Decide

Lean toward do when:
- the team is overwhelmed. It might be time to roll up your sleeves and lend a hand with the work.
- you have new team members. Maybe you need to do some of the work as you get them onboarded and help succeed with the core work first.

Lean toward delegate when:
- you have team members who need a new challenge.
- you have people you are grooming for promotion or want the development new work can provide.
- you have new responsibilities of your own and need some help with your existing work.

- team membership has changed. With new roles come opportunities to train and delegate more work.

This is another Flexor that is more individually situational and doesn't always require the Context Map.

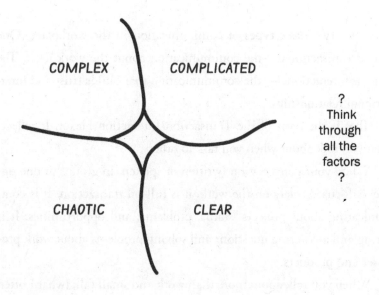

An Example

You have something you would like to delegate, but you know it will take time to hand it off effectively. Because of that time commitment, you have continued to do it rather than delegate. Your perspective may change when you realize that delegation is an investment in the other person and their success. Instead of continuing to do the work yourself, you might consider your training and support time as a part of that investment rather than as time wasted.

THE TRANSACTION/INTERACTION FLEXOR

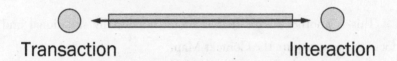

Transaction   Interaction

There are two basic types of communication in the workplace. One type is transactional—the communication about the work itself. The other is interactional—the communication that builds trust and interpersonal relationships.

That is the basis of the Transaction/Interaction Flexor. It reflects what you talk about when you talk to others.

When your conversation (written or spoken, in groups or one-on-one) is focused solely on the work, it is full-on transaction. It is communicating about projects, status, problems, and opportunities. It is asking and answering questions and solving problems about work processes and products.

When you talk about more than work and small talk (what I often call "the work and the weather"), you are having an interaction—finding connections, checking in on people's weekends, asking about their kids, vacations, hopes, and dreams. Interaction can run from everyday interpersonal stuff to career development goals and aspirations.

The Impacts at the Ends

Sometimes leaders say they want to make sure all conversations at work are work conversations. They feel there is no place (or time) at work for fraternization or friendships. That is the perspective at the left end of the Flexor. While this might sound good to you in principle, when you read those two lines, ask yourself: If you had a choice, would you choose a leader whose every conversation with you was transactional?

At the other extreme are leaders who secretly (or maybe not so secretly) want to form friendships with all their team members. These leaders might feel too chummy, share too much, and try too hard to be a part of the friend group at work. Interaction for the sake of interaction (or with mixed goals) isn't very helpful either.

When to Apply It

If there are never any one-on-one interactions, it will be a pretty cold workplace. Even if, as a leader, you don't want to build close relationships at work, chances are you want your team members to form those bonds. Your position on this Flexor will be an example to the team. If you don't make the time to interact, open up, and talk about things beyond work, the team will be less likely to do that too. If there is never time for the team to interact, and meetings are "all business," you can expect a less open and collaborative team.

In a post-COVID world where more people work virtually (at least some of the time), this may be a more important Flexor now than ever.

How to Decide

Lean toward transaction when:
- the context is Clear. If everyone knows what needs to happen, you can likely get on with the work comments.
- the context is Chaotic. The time for small talk and relationship building isn't when tensions and uncertainty are high, and urgency is paramount.

- the workload is high.
- deadlines are approaching.
- people are stressed about their own workloads. Since you know that, extra time in conversation might cause more stress.

Lean toward interaction when:
- you want to be empathetic.
- you want to consciously build relationships.
- you want to connect on common experiences.
- you want to stay connected on life events or situations.

While when the context is Clear or Chaotic transaction may be enough, like a few others, this is a Pervasive Flexor—where the Context Map doesn't fully describe the situation you must consider when flexing. In this case, the context includes the individual, culture, and your desires as a leader too.

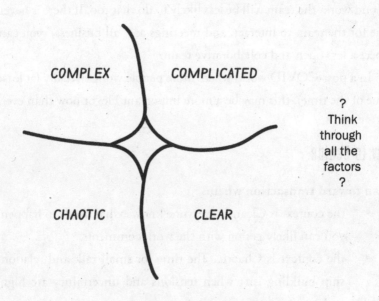

An Example

I lead a team that has been nearly all virtual for over a decade. When people join our team, there is a very important interactional component to their onboarding. Within the first two weeks, each new person is expected to have a 30-minute conversation with each of their new teammates about nonwork topics. With this request, I set the expectation that interaction and relationships are important on our team and are part of the work. (I have one of these conversations with each new team member too.)

This is one way I both model and engage in interaction with the intention of keeping our team from becoming too transactional in our conversations.

THE RESULTS/PROCESS FLEXOR

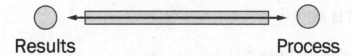

Results   Process

For all work, there is both a what and a how—the result and the process. That is the basis of this Flexor.

Work is usually defined by the results—whether in quality, quantity, sales, revenue, market share, or other factors. Over the past 30 years, organizations have found ways to become more process-aware, from quality and continuous improvement efforts to Lean Six Sigma, to scrums and agile teams. All these efforts and approaches have made us more aware of the process aspects—the *how*—of work.

The Impacts at the Ends

A focus on results can be motivating for you and the team, as it keeps the ultimate objectives clear. However, taken too far, a result-focus can create a "win at all costs" mentality. This can lead to a project-by-project, quarter-by-quarter short-term thinking mentality. Chances are you have seen the downside of this extreme results focus.

A far-right focus on this Flexor helps us step back and look at how things are being done, which is helpful. But the problems start when the process becomes the outcome rather than remembering that the process supports the desired results. Consider Goodhart's law, which states, "When a measure becomes a target it ceases to be a good measure."[27] A full-on process focus can lead to improving processes for their own sake, not considering the 80/20 rule, and as a result lead to confusion or reduced efficiency or productivity.

When to Apply It

Here's the short answer:

When results are disappointing, consider the process. While that might not be the cause of the shortfall, it could be. And remember that you likely have greater influence on the process than you do on the result.

And when you seem lost in the process, step back and look at the results. Ask yourself if you are spending time fixing or improving something that is meaningful and making a difference.

How to Decide

Lean toward results when:

- the context is Chaotic. Focus on stabilizing the system and creating next steps before stepping back to analyze the process problems that might have led to the moment of urgency.
- things are going well. While you must remain vigilant, double down on your current success.
- you have a short-term objective. When you have a short-term goal like creating a new marketing plan, you will likely be better off completing the plan than looking at your planning process.
- your process is proven and the situation is stable.

Lean toward process when:

- the context is Complicated. Ask yourself if your process allows enough experience and expertise to be valued and heard.
- the context is Complex. Make sure your process allows for time to review, test, and try. But make sure you aren't imposing a known process on situations with paradox and uncertainty. Great processes aren't great when applied to the wrong situation.
- you have recurring problems. There is a good chance that looking at your processes will help you find causes and solutions.

Here's a visual simplification:

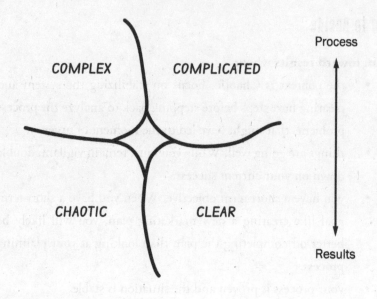

An Example

Meetings are a perfect example of when we can benefit from looking at the Results/Process Flexor. Chances are you have been frustrated by the experience and results of many meetings. When looking at the frustrations people share about meetings, they either fall into results or process issues.

Results frustration includes: "Nothing gets accomplished" (or "We don't know what we are supposed to accomplish") and "We work on the same issues over and over." And process frustrations include not having an agenda, meetings taking too long, people dominating the conversation, and more.

The good news is that when you think about and apply process improvements to meetings, you will often get better results.

THE WITHHOLD/SHARE FLEXOR

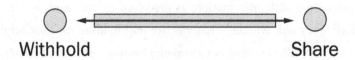

Withhold   **Share**

You could call the Withhold/Share Flexor the Transparency Flexor. In the last 20 years, transparency in leadership has come to be seen as a necessary characteristic of the best leaders. But what does it mean?

When I think of something being transparent, I think of Saran Wrap—the clear film we use in the kitchen to help preserve foods or cover a bowl. It is completely see-through.

If, as leaders, we try to hold ourselves to that standard, it can be really scary.

Does transparency mean sharing everything we know, everything we have done, and everything we are thinking?

Everything is a lot.

Which is one reason why some leaders focus on withholding information to maintain a sense of control, and maybe even to hold more power.

After all, you've heard it said that knowledge is power.

A guest on my *Remarkable Leadership Podcast* once said something incredibly valuable on the show. She said that being transparent gets easier when we distinguish the difference between personal and private. She suggested that we don't need to share what is wholly private, but it is to our advantage to share some personal information.

I believe this distinction is important and helpful and can guide us in our movement on this Flexor.

This Flexor also challenges us to think about what we withhold and share in terms of organizational news and information, not just on the individual dimension. Both are important, and both matter.

The Impacts at the Ends

If you share too little information, as perceived by the team, how will they feel? They will wonder what you are withholding, or they might think you have ulterior (and not altruistic) motives. Trust will be negatively impacted—even if their perception is inaccurate.

But if you share everything, you run the risk of confusion. Part of the role of a leader is to sift, sort, and prioritize information. If you ever feel overwhelmed with the information you have, recognize that if you share it all, your team will be even more overwhelmed. Does that outcome best serve the team and the work?

When to Apply It

Any time new information comes your way, you need to consider how it serves the team to share it, or if it is better to hold it back—at least for now.

If you share it, will it be helpful? If you don't share it, will it cause problems now or later?

Your discernment on this Flexor can be more helpful to your team than you might initially realize.

How to Decide

Lean toward withhold when:
- the information is sensitive.
- the information isn't yet complete.
- there isn't context to help people use or value the information.
- the information could lead to unnecessary, incorrect, or premature worries or concerns.

Lean toward share when:

- the context is Complicated or Complex. Sharing what you do know can help the team move forward on the best course of action.
- the level of anxiety on the team is high. Sharing something to help them see the future or calm any misconceptions might be the best thing to do, even if the information is still incomplete.
- the information you have can give people a new or better perspective on a situation.
- your experience—both successes and especially failures—can increase trust and reduce worry and anxiety.
- you have something to share. Sometimes people assume you do when you really don't.

This is another of the Pervasive Flexors where the situational flexing is about more factors than just the Context Map.

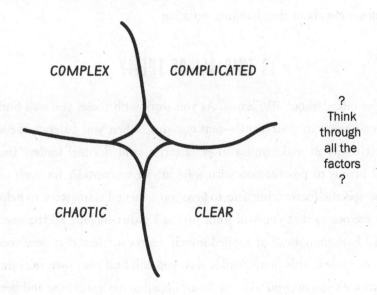

An Example

One of the major times when this Flexor will surface is when you are leading a larger organizational change—especially early in the process. Your team may assume you know more than you let on and wonder why you aren't sharing it. Their assumptions may be true, but perhaps you have been told not to share yet, or there are other considerations keeping you from sharing everything. What do you do in that case?

In my experience, you balance this Flexor by telling people you will tell them what you know when you can tell them. And that you will share as soon as you can. This may be a time where you can share things that squelch rumors, even if you can't say everything yet. This is a case where you are balancing the Withhold/Share Flexor perhaps daily.

This Flexor can help you stay clear and be as transparent as possible with your team. Your openness about your decision-making process may build trust with the team, even though they wish they had more information about the changing situation.

IS THIS ALL OF THEM?

We've talked about 19 Flexors. As you work with these, you will find other Flexors in your work—tensions that, when you balance them effectively, will make you a more effective (and flexible) leader. The goal here is to provide you with solid advice to consider for each of these specific Flexors, but also to give you a mental framework to help you see others that you will find. Just as I didn't include all the ones that I have thought of or applied myself, I am confident that once you see your role in this more flexible way, you will find your own relevant Flexors. As you do, you will now be equipped to navigate those and flex more effectively.

PAUSE AND REFLECT

Before you move on, take a minute to think about these questions. (Even better if you take some notes on your thoughts!)

- Which of these Flexors caused me to pause or created the biggest aha moment for me?
- Where will I gain impact by flexing differently today?
- What are some recent situations where I might have gotten better results if I had flexed differently?

RESOURCES TO HELP YOU LEAD FLEXIBLY

You can get a pocket fast guide to the Flexors at FlexibleLeadership-Book.com or by scanning this QR code.

> . . . remember that the art of Flexible Leadership is remembering that success is rarely at the extreme ends of the Flexor spectrum but will often lie somewhere between those extremes. Your intention and the context of the situation will help you find where to land within the center band.

SECTION 3

THE HABITSET OF FLEXIBLE LEADERS

> We are what we repeatedly do. Excellence, then, is not an
> act, but a habit.
>
> —Will Durant, historian and philosopher[28]

Mindset and awareness are important precursors to any change we want to make. If you aren't aware of the need to change, you will be blissfully unaware and likely resting in your comfort zone. If you don't see things in new ways, you will be effectively blind. When that happens, the status quo wins.

Hopefully at this point you have a new mindset and awareness—that even if you have been relatively successful as a leader so far, you can still reach new heights and have a bigger positive impact.

But mindset isn't enough. In fact, without knowing what to do to change, without having skills to apply to the situation, you won't change either. You might be uncomfortable with the present state and yearn for something more, but if you don't know how to change, you won't. Without the needed skills, change won't happen.

Section 2 gave you the tool kit: the skillset. You have the skills available to you via the Flexors. But something is still missing.

But (and this is a big *but . . .*)

Have you ever left a workshop excited and ready to try your new skills, but then you didn't incorporate them into your work the way you planned?

That is why this section on your habitset is needed and so important. If you are excited (or even simply intrigued) by what you have read so far, don't stop now. Because what is still to come is critical to your ultimate success as a Flexible Leader.

CHAPTER 10

BEYOND THE FORMULA

What first separates a leader from a normal human being?
A leader knows who they are as a human being.

—Stan Slap, author[29]

At this point, you have the full picture of the Flexible Leadership Model. You understand the roles of intention, context, and Flexors. But getting there requires us to look at a few things beyond the formula. Without acknowledging, understanding, and applying these ideas, you will be stuck.

Stuck in the space of wanting to be a more flexible leader, but not being able or willing to do it. Stuck with knowledge and skills but no action.

This chapter will help you avoid or overcome that uncomfortable and unhelpful state.

LEADERSHIP STYLE

A quick Google search on "how many types of leadership styles are there" gave me a wide assortment of answers, including: 24, 11, 9, 8, and 6. And this was just on the first page of the results. Each of these models likely has an assessment or approach to determine your style, further validating it in the minds of those who use it.

Because leadership is so important and valuable, people have been trying to understand and categorize it since at least the 1840s. Here's the evolution in perhaps the shortest form you will ever read.

- *Traits.* We can determine leadership effectiveness by traits. In the 1840s, the Great Man Theory implied that leaders were born. This theory says that innate traits determine leadership success. By the 1930s and 1940s, the focus was on personality traits and qualities. The point was that if we can define those traits, leaders can learn them.
- *Behaviors.* In the 1940s and 1950s, the focus shifted to behaviors that can be learned. This gave rise to leadership style assessments and is the foundation of many leadership development efforts even today.
- *Situational.* In the 1960s, thinking shifted to how leaders could respond to a context and choose a style based on the situation. (This may sound familiar—it is connected to the foundation of Flexible Leadership.)
- *Transactional and transformational.* In the 1990s and 2000s, two overarching theories emerged: transactional leadership, which relies on authority and position to motivate, and transformational leadership, which focuses on encouraging, inspiring, and motivating followers.

You clearly see these ideas inside of most any text you read on leadership. All are part of how we see and understand leadership. But taken in total, it reinforces what we already know: leadership is complex and hard to put our arms around.

When things are complex, smart people create models to simplify the complexity, with the goal of helping us navigate it. Peter Northouse, in the ninth edition of his book *Leadership: Theory and Practice*, reports, "In the last 60 years, as many as 65 different leadership classification systems have been developed to define the dimensions of leadership."[30]

Sixty-five systems.

Most with multiple styles associated with them.

All with a wonderful goal.

And all with major downsides.

When we use a model to simplify the complex, we can create insights. Models give us clues about the complex whole, but in simplifying to create the model, nuance is lost. And what once was meant to be a helpful aid becomes a rigid box, reinforced by pattern recognition.

While these models and styles can be very helpful as tools for understanding, at their worst, whichever model you use, whichever assessment you have taken, they can lead you to incorporate your style as a part of who you are.

You are more than a style, a strength, or a type.

If you want to lead with the highest impact, you must recognize models as tools, not explanations or excuses.

To be a Flexible Leader requires us to step beyond the explanations and comfort of being a facilitative, servant, visionary, strategic, democratic, autocratic, coaching, or transformational leader. It challenges us to recognize our strengths, attributes, and natural tendencies but not let them define or limit us.

IDENTITY

If you identify with a style or type, it can get in your way.

If you see yourself as a servant leader, you will look for ways to serve.

If you see yourself as a democratic leader, you will focus on getting wide input.

If you see yourself as a coaching leader, you will look for chances to coach and frame problems as coaching opportunities.

And the more closely you associate with that style as a part of who you are, the more you resist changing it.

It's why you listen to a band's third or fourth album and think it is good but can easily identify their style and approach (and it hasn't really changed much).

It's why the cook stays with their tried-and-true recipes.

It's why the "old school" leader complains about the new generation in the workplace.

But it doesn't have to be so. Taylor Swift, the mom who is always trying new recipes, and the boss who constantly adjusts are examples of reframing success and identity.

Until you are ready to reframe your identity to being a Flexible Leader, you will struggle more than you need to.

How do you make the shift? Here are some examples.

- "I'm a servant leader" can become "I lead by serving the situation in ways that bring us success."
- "I'm a democratic leader" can become "I get input when the situation warrants but am confident in my ideas too."
- "I'm a coaching leader" can become "I use coaching as a tool to help the team grow and succeed."

When you consider yourself flexible, you identify and adapt to the changing context and circumstances. Water has power in part because of its ability to flow around obstacles. The quote from the *Tao Te Ching* (and suggested by James Clear in *Atomic Habits*) makes the point beautifully:

Men are born soft and supple;
Dead they are stiff and hard.
Plants are born tender and pliant;
Dead they are brittle and dry.
Thus whoever is stiff and inflexible
Is a disciple of death.
Whoever is soft and yielding
Is a disciple of life.
The hard and stiff will be broken.
The soft and supple will prevail.

WHERE TO START

Once you have decided (i.e., changed your intention) that Flexible Leadership is an approach that will benefit you, your team, and your organization, what's next?

Here are five things you can do that will help you with the transition from skills and desire to results:

- Look at your resistance.
- Determine your Starter Flexors.
- Identify exemplars.
- Review the framework.
- Move from VUCA to FICO.

Let's look at each in some detail.

Look at Your Resistance

As you read through the Flexors in the previous chapters, there were some that probably made you bristle or resist a bit more than others. You might have disagreed with what you read or wanted to justify yourself. These "resistors" are likely the Flexors you need to focus on first.

Why?

Because your mental dialogue is pointing you to your tendency (at one end of the spectrum or the other). That is a sign that those are Flexors you likely don't flex on often. It may be associated with a style or a part of how you view your role as a leader, and therefore probably is a blind spot. If one or more Flexors stand out for you in this way, you have identified your Starter Flexors.

Determine Your Starter Flexors

Even if you want to, you can't apply all of the Flexors immediately—if you try that, you will become overwhelmed, frustrated, and unsuccessful. Your resistance may have highlighted your Starter Flexors already. If so, great. If not, pick one to start with that intrigues you, you hadn't thought of before, or you see personal opportunity with. Look for situations to intentionally slide across that spectrum based on the situation and context you face. Don't overcomplicate it to start; just stop and look at situations and ask yourself this general question:

**Which direction should I lean in to get better results
for everyone (both now and in the future)?**

Then act on your answer rather than doing what you might have done automatically. Once you become able to flex that Flexor, you are building the Flexible Leadership habit.

FIND YOUR EXEMPLARS

While improvement requires practice, you can learn and grow through observation too. Exemplars are people you see as role models to help you build skill and confidence. I recommend you find two exemplars for leadership flexibility—people who give you a picture of the skills and success you want.

- Someone who seems able to flex their leadership style in general (whether they have read the book or not)
- Someone who is especially good on the other end of your Starter Flexor

In both cases you can observe them and reflect on what you might have done that was different from their approach. Beyond observing, if possible, ask to sit down with them and have them share their approaches and success with their specific tendencies. Again, they don't have to have read this book for you to learn from them. (Maybe you can give them a copy as a gift for their time.)

Review the Framework

The Context Map will take some time to integrate into your thinking. Reviewing the summary of the framework (see next page) regularly will help it become a part of your thinking more rapidly—and make it easier to apply the formula.

UNORDERED   ORDERED

COMPLEX

- There are unknown unknowns
- Competing ideas
  and opinions exist
- Things are unpredictable
  and unstable
- Paradox and contradictions exist
- Need for ideas and innovation

COMPLICATED

- There are knowns and unknowns
- We can forecast or guess
  but it is hard to definitely know
- Experts are needed
- Situational analysis needed

CHAOTIC

- There are unknowables!
- High turbulence and tension
- No patterns seem to exist
- No time to think
- Many decisions to make . . .
  now

CLEAR

- The knowns are known
- Familiar and known patterns
- Wide agreement on cause and effect
- We have the facts
  and they are indisputable
- Obvious and agreed-on solutions

Move from VUCA to FICO

VUCA (which stands for volatility, uncertainty, complexity, and ambiguity) is an acronym first described by Warren Bennis and Burt Nanus in their book *Leaders: Strategies for Taking Charge*.[31] It was popularized in the 1990s by the US Army War College after the collapse of the Soviet Union and the end of the Cold War. It makes sense. Think about how things were at that time:

- Volatile
- Uncertain
- Complex
- Ambiguous

And they still are today.

But rather than wringing our hands or wishing for easier times, as Flexible Leaders we must acknowledge VUCA and counteract it with FICO:

- Flexible
- Intentional
- Contextual
- Opportunistic

You have a FICO credit score, which measures your creditworthiness. In the world of Flexible Leadership, your FICO score measures your ability and willingness to respond to the VUCA world we live in.

PAUSE AND REFLECT

Before you move on, take a minute to think about these questions. (Even better if you take some notes on your thoughts!)

- What (if any) leadership styles do I identify with?
- Are they a part of my identity to a degree that they get in my way?
- What is my Starter Flexor, and why?
- Who are the exemplars that can be role models for me?

When we use a model to simplify the complex, we can create insights. Models give us clues about the complex whole, but in simplifying to create the model, nuance is lost. And what once was meant to be a helpful aid becomes a rigid box, reinforced by pattern recognition.

CHAPTER 11

WHAT DOESN'T FLEX

You will find that if you will always stand for what's right,
your self-confidence will increase. The more you stand for
your values, the easier it will become to stand against the
pressures of life. Soon, you will become a rock that cannot
be moved, even in the greatest storms.

—Bohdi Sanders, author[32]

I opened the book with the paradox of flexibility as a leader. I said that being a Flexible Leader requires both/and rather than either/or thinking. And hopefully, I have done a good job of helping you see a picture of why flexibility is a core leadership mindset, skillset, and habitset.

Flexible Leadership is *how* we lead.

But what doesn't change?

I mentioned my definition of leadership in chapter 1, *leadership is reaching valuable outcomes with and through others*, and we have talked about the Outcomes/Others Flexor.

There are always outcomes you are trying to reach. Those goals and outcomes will change based on your role, organization, and situation.

But as a leader, there will always be outcomes you are responsible for.

That is what you are being paid to accomplish. These overarching outcomes are why we are leading.

We can and must flex to reach them, but those desired outcomes as defined by organizational need and strategy are what we are leading toward.

What those outcomes are might change, but the fact that outcomes are critical to our role as leaders is unchanging.

The fact that there are outcomes to reach won't change, and the fact that you aren't doing it alone—but with others—won't change either.

And there will always be others involved. If you are working alone, you aren't leading; you are just working. Who those others are will change, but not the fact that there are others!

Outcomes and others are the *what* of leadership.

And that doesn't change.

There is a third *O* in the 3O Model of Leadership in chapter 1. Here it is again.

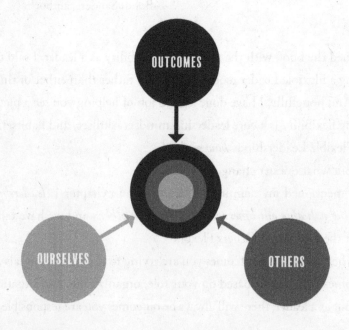

The *ourselves* part of the model reminds us that who we are as a leader plays a huge role in how we impact outcomes and others.

You are *the who* of leadership.

And how we lead (hopefully more flexibly) isn't who we are. Previously, we have talked about how identity can get in the way of us adjusting and changing our approach. But identity still plays a valuable role in our ability to lead effectively when we frame it accurately.

The song I learned and sang in Sunday school (don't ask me about the hand motions), based on a parable in the Bible, is instructive here—the first two verses in particular:

> The wise man built his house upon the rock, the wise man built his house upon the rock, and the rains came tumbling down.
>
> The rains came down and the floods came up, the rains came down, and the floods came up, but the house on the rock stood firm.

This chapter is about what stays rock-solid: what doesn't flex as the rains, uncertainties, challenges, complexities, and volatilities come.

That foundation is your identity, who you are at the core. Let's explore three parts of the foundation of who we are—what truly defines us. Once the foundation of who we are is firm, we can flex on how we lead far more easily and confidently.

YOUR PURPOSE

Why do you lead?

Why do you care about doing the hard and sometimes frustrating work of leading?

While you might not have perfect answers to this question, if you are still reading 11 chapters in, I am confident you have thought about it.

Your purpose is part of your personal foundation from which you can lead more effectively. Even if the approaches you take are flexible, the reason you are leading in the first place shouldn't be.

If your purpose isn't clear, or is imminently selfish, there is already a cap on your leadership potential.

What do I mean by "imminently selfish"?

Look at the 3O Model again on page 168. If the only circle that matters to you is the "ourselves" circle—if you don't truly care about the "outcomes or others" but see them as a stepping stone to personal glory and success—you have a selfish and cynical view of the role and responsibility. If you see being a leader as simply and solely an opportunity for you to reach your personal goals and objectives, people will eventually see through your intentions and your effectiveness, and your success will be diminished.

If you want to make your purpose clearer and your foundation stronger, here are some questions (along with those mentioned earlier) to help you think through them:

- When is it easy for you to lead others?
- What fills you emotionally?
- What are you doing when you get your best ideas and solutions?
- When do you feel most satisfied and fulfilled?
- What are you doing when you feel at your best?

(Thanks to Pete Steinberg and his book *Leadership Shock* for inspiration and help with these questions.)

YOUR PRINCIPLES

Your leadership principles are the things that are true for you as a leader. They define how you want to lead, help you deal with challenging times, and hold you accountable for your actions. These are your most deeply held beliefs about leading.

Here are a few of mine:

- Leadership is about outcomes and others—and both are critical to my success.
- Committed, engaged, and accountable individuals and teams can accomplish great things.
- Seeing and enhancing potential is my job.
- Flexibility in approach leads to better leadership outcomes.

I share them not for you to adopt them, but as examples. There are a couple of things to note about them:

- They are evergreen—and can guide and hold us accountable always.
- They are not aspirational—they are true today.
- They are about more than us, but about the work and the team.
- Flexibility is one of the principles.

Time spent clarifying and codifying your principles will help make your leadership foundation stronger. I encourage you to think about these and use the criteria here to help you. Lastly, I hope that one of your principles will now include flexibility.

YOUR VALUES

Here is what I said about values in my book *Remarkable Leadership*: "Your values are those ideas, beliefs, and concepts that you hold most dear and guide your behavior daily."

Our values do guide our behavior but also reveal it. While I encourage you to have a clear and stated list of values (more on that in a minute), your real ones are those you live out each day. Any disconnect between what you say and what you do is a problem.

Maybe you have experienced this disconnect in an organization. There may be a written culture or values statement, but the actual behavior in that workplace is different from what is written on the website or posted in the hallway or conference rooms. Which are the real values?

The ones you observe are the real ones.

We are human and will sometimes choose or do things that don't perfectly align with our values. But the more clearly you can state them, the more likely they will reflect who you are most of the time.

This may not be the first book you have read that suggested you think about your values and write them down. You may have attended a workshop that suggested the same thing. Whether you have heard this before or not, doing it seems like a good idea.

There are several reasons why people who would like to have a written list of values never start. Here are the three I hear most often:

- It takes time and thought.
- It feels like a test—like I have to get them right.
- I don't know how to start.

I can't help with the first one, except to agree. It will take time and effort. And, like most valuable things in life, it will be worth the effort.

I personally identify with the second reason, because that is how I felt about writing this book (and, to a large degree, all the others I have written). When the pressure you put on yourself to get it right is high, you may procrastinate (I know I do). But just like with a book, we don't have to get it right the first time. Think of identifying your values not as a test, but as an iterative process. You can make a list, then edit, adjust, and change it until you get it right—just like I have done with this book.

Getting started at lots of things can be hard. Staring at a blank sheet of paper without a path forward can be daunting. Writer's block is real. That's why I have included our suggested values creation process and a "cheat sheet"—a list of potential values to help you brainstorm and get started. Details about how to get this list and use it to create a draft of your values are at the end of the chapter.

But here is a sampling. If I gave you 15 random values from that list, like these . . .

- Accountability
- Adaptability
- Commitment
- Courage
- Empathy
- Gratitude
- Humility
- Innovation
- Integrity
- Patience
- Resilience
- Respect
- Service

- Transparency
- Vision

. . . you would likely nod your head that those are all desirable. But some are more meaningful, personal, and important to you. Those would more likely make your short list of values to further contemplate and sort through.

NOW WHAT?

You might be thinking, *Will the effort of writing these out be worth it?* Intellectually, it might make sense to you, but if you don't have an application for them, what is the point? It is a valid question to ask—*What will I do with these?*

Your written purpose, principles, and values, even when they are works in progress, are some of the most important things you will ever document. I encourage you to keep them near you and easily accessible. I find that referring to them regularly is a great practice to keep me grounded and inspired to lead as my best self. That regular refresher is also when you might tweak the wording and continue to move them closer to being "perfect" for you.

When there are storms and challenges, these three lists can be your compass and your comfort too. Just as a sailor relies on their compass to get their bearings and continue on their desired path, your purpose, principles, and values can do the same for you in times of struggle and significant complexity.

The sailor adjusts the sails but doesn't change the destination.

Your path may change regularly as you lead your team or organization. But knowing your foundation and outcome allows you to flex the things that do flex far more effectively.

PAUSE AND REFLECT

Before you move on, take a minute to think about these questions. (Even better if you take some notes on your thoughts!)

- Is my purpose clear? (If not, when will I spend some time on the questions in the Purpose section on page 169?)
- What are the principles that guide who I am as a leader?
- Which of the 15 values listed on page 173 are most meaningful to me?

RESOURCES TO HELP YOU LEAD FLEXIBLY

You can get the starter list of values and value creation process at FlexibleLeadershipBook.com or by scanning this QR code.

Your purpose is part of your personal foundation from which you can lead more effectively. Even if the approaches you take are flexible, the reason you are leading in the first place shouldn't be.

CHAPTER 12

TURNING SKILL TO HABIT

> Success is the sum of small efforts repeated day in and
> day out.
>
> —Robert Collier, author[33]

This is perhaps the most important chapter in the book.

How do you overcome your habits, auto-responses, beliefs, and biases? How do you know when to apply the skillset of Flexible Leadership?

Your habitset.

That's what we are going to explore in this chapter.

To help us turn skill into habit, we will reframe learning and look at research on habits and rituals. In the process, you will see how to turn your new awareness and tools into living, breathing Flexible Leadership.

THE KNOWING-DOING GAP

As a person who has developed and delivered tons of training in a variety of forms over more than 30 years, I know there is something important to mention here.

Training is one way we can learn, but it can only take us so far. For years, we have told prospects, clients, and participants that *training is an event, but learning is a process*. So, while training is one of the services we provide, we know its value is necessarily limited.

Why?

Because *knowing* something is very different from *doing* something.

Training can provide awareness and knowledge. But if we want different and better performance, behaviors, and results, *knowing* isn't enough. We must act on what we have learned.

Why do I share that with you?

Because at this point, if you have read everything up until now, it is sort of like having attended a workshop. You have some new ways of looking at things. You have some new ideas. You (hopefully) are excited about what you have learned. You have a new mindset and a new skillset.

But you don't completely know how to apply those skills, when to apply those skills, and how to overcome . . . yourself.

In your quest to become a more flexible leader, you must reframe the finish line. The finish line is leading more effectively, which means we must get through application, not just gain knowledge.

Helping leaders close this "knowing-doing" gap is frustrating as a designer, speaker, trainer, and facilitator, and even more so as an author. That is why I am including this chapter—to give you some guidance and encouragement, and to keep you from stopping short of putting the ideas in this book to work.

Beyond the general wisdom of closing the knowing-doing gap, I think it is especially important for the mindset, skillset, and habitset of Flexible Leadership for these five reasons:

- Our more complex world of work requires us to step up to a level of leadership beyond where most of us have led.

- The skills we have talked about in some cases go against your prevailing beliefs and past successes.
- The intention needed will require you to slow down at times—which seems counterintuitive.
- The context tools we have talked about might be truly new thinking for you.
- The Flexible Leadership Approach requires that we know when to adjust.

HOW TO CREATE FLEXIBLE LEADERSHIP HABITS

Much has been discovered in the last 30 years about how habits are formed and changed. *Atomic Habits* by James Clear is the most popular of the books that have brought this research and knowledge about brain function and human behavior to a wider audience. If you haven't read this book, I highly encourage it to further help you lock in the changes you want to make to lead more effectively. One of my favorite lines in the book is: "Habits are the compound interest of self-improvement."[34]

The Power of Compound Interest

You know how powerful compound interest is (Einstein called it "the most powerful idea in the world"). The additional interest added is then part of the basis for the next interest. If you invest $1,000 at 6% interest, in a year you will have $1,060. But in 12 years, your money would double.

Just like this financial example, when you start building new habits (including those we are talking about in this book), it will be slow at first, and it won't look like you are making a lot of progress. But when you continue to improve with the effects of the habits building on themselves, and look back at it later, you will be amazed by the growth. And if we repeat a habit daily, it is like compounding interest daily (rather than annually, like in the investment example). Let's say you just improve 1% a day. If you do that every day, in a year you will be about 37 times better than you were at the start.

Regardless of your starting point as a leader, if you changed your habits to support a 1% improvement per day, week, or even month, while you might not notice much change at first, you will be a significantly more effective leader far sooner than you imagined.

Layers of Behavioral Change

In chapter 2 of *Atomic Habits*, Clear talks about the three layers of behavioral change, and they are especially applicable to the work you are doing to become a more effective Flexible Leader. Those layers are:

- *Changing your outcomes.* Since you are reading these words, you are (at least) here. Your goal is to be a more effective leader—you want to have a greater impact. Goals like these are examples of the *outcome layer* of behavioral change.
- *Changing your process.* This book provides ideas about what you need to change in terms of approaches, systems, and habits. Consider this the *habit layer*.
- *Changing your identity.* While habits help us change behavior, if the behavior is a mismatch with our beliefs, we may never be fully successful. This is the *identity layer*. If, even after reading this book and trying to apply the ideas in it, you see yourself as a facilitative, servant, or collaborative leader (rather than a Flexible Leader), you will make little significant change to your behaviors (and therefore your performance and results).

When the habits we build are focused on who we want to become (identity) rather than on processes or outcomes, the chances that the new habits last are far higher.

We aren't trying to be Flexible Leaders; we *are* Flexible Leaders—and this is what they do. This is the ultimate source of intrinsic motivation.

The Habit Spiral

Multiple authors have popularized the idea of the habit loop or cycle. I like to think of it as a spiral—and since we are talking about adding positive habits, we'll think in terms of an upward spiral. Consider this spiral as an endless feedback loop that creates automatic habits. The more times we loop, the more automatic the habit becomes. If the habit helps us, the spiral moves upward (hello, compound interest!). If the habit doesn't ultimately help us, we set ourselves up to be automatically doing things that don't serve our best interests or results. Here are the four parts in this loop or spiral, using a common example:

Cue	Someone walks into your office and asks a question.
Craving	You want to help them (and perhaps get back to what you were doing).
Response	You answer their question.
Reward	You feel good about solving the problem and getting back to your work.

When you read this very common situation, perhaps you see you could do something different with this situation that might get you a better result, even though this is your automatic response. (Don't worry, this is the overwhelming habit of most leaders.) It could look different. Here's another example that takes a far more flexible approach.

Cue	Someone walks into your office and asks a question.
Craving	You want them to improve and be more confident (and maybe not interrupt as often).
Response	You ask them what they have considered or tried so far, or perhaps what they would recommend themselves.
Reward	You feel good about helping them engage, learn, and grow. You also know you may now be interrupted less—or only interrupted when it is most needed.

All our behavior is aimed at solving problems. When thinking about the spiral, the first two parts are the problem, and the second two parts are the solution. You likely know how profoundly true this statement is: *How we define the problem points us to the solution.* This is clear in the examples. The craving, or the problem we are trying to solve, sets the table for the solution: the response and reward.

As a Flexible Leader, you now have a new craving in many situations. You now crave the best outcome based on the context, not the one you are most comfortable or familiar with. The Flexors give you ways to think about your cues differently, but to make new automatic habits, you have to stop long enough to consider the cues and cravings you have used for years.

In *Atomic Habits*, Clear gives us questions to help change our loop or spiral:

- How can I make the cue more obvious?
- How can I make the craving more attractive?
- How can I make the response easier?
- How can I make the reward more satisfying?

With the Flexible Leadership Mindset and Approach, you already have good answers to the last three questions. It is the first one that is most important for us to create the flexible habits we need. Specifically:

How do we see that we might need to be more flexible in the moment? How do we slow down enough to check context in the cue, rather than using our existing pattern recognition to assume a most likely Clear context?

Awareness

For us to change our habits, we must be aware of our current ones. If you review your mental approach in a given situation and write down what your responses tend to look like, it will be far easier to see what you could (or want to) change. Without awareness of the cue, you can't reframe the craving, and you will "rinse and repeat" what you have done in the past without even thinking.

You can do this for anything, but I would begin with the Starter Flexors you have identified. The situations/cues in those Flexor moments are likely the first ones you will want to "reprogram" for your Habit Spiral.

When you do this analysis, you will see that the habit is effective based on the problem you are trying to solve. After you have this list of steps documented, considering the goals you have to lead more flexibly, the problem will be reframed and you can determine and document the new steps you want to eventually become your new norm.

THE ROLE OF RITUAL

You will not change your approach and results as a leader without consciously working to build more effective habits or automatic responses. But because the concept and approach of Flexible Leadership is so different and counterintuitive to many, we need another tool as well.

That tool is ritual.

While rituals can be societal or group based and are often connected to religion or beliefs (think marriages, baptisms, or bar/bat mitzvahs), they can also be more personal and not have a religious connection.

While changing habits requires us to refine our intention and desire up front, rituals serve a bigger-picture purpose. You could look at rituals as a mega-habit. But my purpose in differentiating them is an application of the Details / Big Picture Flexor.

Rituals are a big-picture activity; habits are the details. Like all Flexors, we need both to be most successful. The amount of each we need (in this case, rituals and habits) depends on our own leadership path.

If you struggle with the big picture of Flexible Leadership or your current beliefs (identity) are deeply ingrained, then this section on ritual might be more helpful to you. And if you have habits that are automatic, but you now see them as counter to your goal of being more flexible, your work on habits might need to take precedence.

Ryder Carroll, in his Medium article titled "Habit vs. Ritual," states the difference beautifully, and directly to our point.

Though routines and rituals share many of the same means, what is often lost, is that their ends are very different. Whereas the goal of a routine is to make a behavior automatic, the goal of a ritual is to make it intentional.[35]

The first component of the Flexible Leadership Approach is intention. If we don't hold that intention as a general belief and starting point, our ability to get the results we want will be severely limited.

Casper ter Kuile, in his book *The Power of Ritual: Turning Everyday Activities into Soulful Practices*, suggests that rituals needn't be religious, but they may well be spiritual, at least to the individual. He says, "I've come to believe that just about anything can *become* a spiritual practice—gardening, painting, singing, sitting. The world is full of these rituals."[36]

Here are three of my personal rituals:

- If you were observing me when I am on our farm (where I grew up), you would see me walking around, especially behind the buildings in the field, and you would think I am just walking. But I'm doing something more. When I am on that walk, I am reconnecting with my kidhood. I am reflecting on the memories—good and bad—that I have of nearly every square foot of that property. I am connecting with my long-departed father. This walk fills my emotional reserves. It isn't "just a walk"; it is a ritual. I am better, more intentional, more grounded, and more connected when I repeat that ritual.

- I have written email newsletters for many years. As I write this, I have written an issue of our weekly *Unleashing Your Remarkable Potential* newsletter* for 1,018 consecutive weeks.

---

* You can subscribe to the newsletter at KevinEikenberry.com/newsletters.

Writing new content as a part of that process each week is a task. But most weeks, I see it as more than just a task—I see it as an important part of who I am and a connection of my work to my personal purpose and our organizational mission. It isn't just a task; it is a ritual.

- Ask my team, and they will tell you. When I have a new idea, or when something important is about to happen, I rub my hands together quickly, and if the situation allows, I end with a clap. This strange behavior is a ritual for me too. It helps me build my energy and passion in that moment, and it makes me more optimistic and opportunity focused. (By the way, I did it before I sat down to write this section.)

I share these as examples, not as things you need to replicate. You hopefully see three things in these examples—they are three components of any ritual according to ter Kuile. Rituals are created by:

- *Intention.* (There is that word again!) When we do something with intention, we have the first part of ritual.
- *Attention.* Note in my examples that an action becomes ritual (and not just a walk or writing task, for example) when attention is paid to it. Ritual, to have real meaning, requires attention to and being present in the moment.
- *Repetition.* Doing something once might be intentional, and you might be present—and it might be very memorable. But great moments or memories alone don't make rituals (or make them powerful); repetition does.

I encourage you to look for examples of rituals you already have in your life to help you see this power. I also encourage you to look for rituals that will inspire and remind you of the power of the practices we are talking about. Rituals (large or small) can help you reframe, remember, and recommit to being a more effective, confident, and flexible leader.

While your mileage will vary and you ultimately need to create your own rituals, I will share three that point you in a helpful direction.

- Spend quiet time thinking and reflecting.
- Spend time reading content that uplifts and inspires you.
- Spend time being grateful.

Maybe you will create rituals around these suggestions. Even if you don't see or use them in that way, they are valuable practices that will help you and reinforce your ability and confidence to lead with more flexibility. Regardless of how you use these ideas, notice that all of them slow us down, change our perspective, and give us input that grants us new energy. Regardless of the rituals you might create, those criteria will be helpful.

DON'T DO IT ALONE

There is no doubt that being a leader is sometimes a lonely role. There are things you can't share or don't feel comfortable sharing with your team members. Many around us don't lead, so they don't have context or experience to help us beyond listening.

And trying to apply new skills can be even harder. If you want to move from mindset to skillset to habitset, you need help. Here are several ways you can get help and support from others:

- *Buy someone the book.* I'm not saying this just to sell more books, even though that sounds good to me. Find someone else who wants to improve as a leader and buy them a copy. Once they have read the book, they can become your learning partner. Now, with a common mindset and skillset, you can help each other grow and apply what you have read. You can listen to, encourage, coach, and help each other be accountable for implementing your new ideas.

- *Work with your coach.* Hopefully your boss serves you as a coach. Perhaps you have an internal or external coach, whether formal or informal. They don't have to have read the book (but hey, buy them copies too!). You can share what you are working on applying and why, and they can be helpful as a sounding board, to ask you great questions, and to help you with accountability.

- *Have an accountability partner.* Either of these first two people can be your accountability partner, but even if you don't have a coach to leverage or a colleague to learn with, you can still get this help. Ask a person close to you to meet with you regularly to simply ask if you are taking the actions you planned and building the habits you want. If your answer is no, their next questions should be: Why not? What is in your way? Knowing that someone cares and will be asking you about your progress makes you far more likely to practice your new skills and build your new habits.

- *Get help from your team.* What would happen if you told your team that you were working on improving in a specific area and that you wanted feedback from them on how you are doing? Would that help you be more accountable? Would it empower them? Would it be sending a powerful message (and model) about learning? Would it build your trust with them? Don't underestimate how much your team can help you in your journey toward being a more flexible leader. After all, they are the recipients of your leadership behaviors and approaches.

PAUSE AND REFLECT

Before you move on, take a minute to think about these questions. (Even better if you take some notes on your thoughts!)

- What habits will I look at and improve first?
- What are three examples of meaningful rituals I use?
- What ritual might I develop to help me be more intentional as a Flexible Leader?
- Who can help me on my path to Flexible Leadership?

> When the habits we build are focused on who we want to become (identity) rather than on processes or outcomes, the chances that the new habits last are far higher.

CHAPTER 13

CREATING AN ORGANIZATION
OF FLEXIBLE LEADERS

Leadership and learning are indispensable to each other.
—John F. Kennedy[37]

When you drop a pebble in a pond, a series of ripples is created. As an individual leader practicing the skills of Flexible Leadership, you are like that pebble.

In an organization, each leader is creating their own set of ripples. Imagine walking up to a pond and throwing a handful of pebbles in at once. Chaos on the surface of the water ensues. The ripples formed by each individual pebble create a churn in the water.

Now imagine a stone of equal weight to the handful of pebbles is tossed into the pond. One set of ripples will extend from the stone. The ripples will be clearer, more powerful, and they will extend farther. The impact of this single stone can even overcome the chaos of choppy water.

The first situation is you as an individual leader getting results based on how you lead.

The second situation shows how your impact as an individual will be muted if others are leading in different ways, with differing levels of impact.

The third situation is an organization leading with a common approach, with the skills to overcome the churn and choppiness and create consistent and powerful ripples of results.

Your results as an individual Flexible Leader will improve and your impact will be enhanced. But the transformation of an organization will accelerate as more of the leaders are transformed themselves.

ARE YOU THINKING ORGANIZATIONALLY?

If you are reading with your organizational hat on—as an HR, talent, OD, L&D, or leadership development professional—this chapter is specifically for you. At this point, you see how the Flexible Leadership Approach can augment and extend the leadership skills of your leaders, but you might be wondering how to get there.

ARE YOU AN INDIVIDUAL LEADER?

If you have been reading this book as an individual leader, you might feel tempted to skip this chapter, but don't. Read on and think about how you can influence the leaders around you and the whole organization. You can have influence beyond your own example, and this chapter will help you think about that in a more concrete way.

THE ROAD MAP

If you believe Flexible Leaders can help you get better organizational results and you want your organization to develop these skills in your leaders, six steps are required:

1. Decide it matters.
2. Get specific.
3. Think context.
4. Think culture.
5. Create learning opportunities.
6. Integrate Flexible Leadership into daily work.

Let's look at each of these in some detail.

Decide It Matters

Until your organization realizes that leadership effectiveness drives better organizational results, one of two things will happen.

- *Nothing.* No investments (whether in the Flexible Leadership Approach or anything else) will occur.
- *Groundhog Day.* Like Bill Murray in the movie, you will keep repeating the same behaviors. This looks like investing in some leadership development training when there is a budget, but not tying it to organizational results or holding people accountable for improvement. As we discussed earlier in the book, that is the insanity approach to leadership development: doing the same thing and expecting different results.

While I am (and have been throughout the book) lobbying for Flexible Leadership mindsets, skillsets, and habitsets, this is a generic point. Until your organization decides to act on developing leaders as an organizational imperative to create better and needed organizational results, little will change.

There is plenty of good advice available on creating a business case for leadership development. While we can't ignore this critical first step, it isn't our focus here. I will assume you know what to do, have a trusted advisor who can help, or will reach out to us for that guidance and assistance (we would be happy to talk with you).

Get Specific

Once the idea of *better leaders = better organizational results* has taken hold, you can get more specific about suggesting/employing the Flexible Leadership Approach in your organization. Use the ideas and concepts in the first couple of chapters to help you share the ideas and importance of greater flexibility in your leaders.

This means you need to explore the role of uncertainty in your organization and help people see that when leading through uncertainty, they must lead differently. This also means you must look at how many assessments and tools you are using that might be confusing or even misleading your leaders. While leadership styles can be helpful as a starting point, if you are encouraging people to lean into these styles as "fact" rather than as one of many data points, you will make it harder to move toward the Flexible Leadership Approach.

Use Context in Conversation and the Work

By now you know that the idea of identifying context is a core part of the Flexible Leadership Approach. That means that the easier we can make it for leaders to be intentionally thinking about context, the more likely they will appropriately flex. One of the ways we can do that is to make the Cynefin Framework common knowledge in the organization.

The more people that understand this framework, the more powerfully the organization can support leaders in leading more flexibly. The more people who understand this summary and why it applies, the more likely leaders will get out of their established System 1 thinking auto-responses.

UNORDERED   **ORDERED**

COMPLEX

- There are unknown unknowns
- Competing ideas and opinions exist
- Things are unpredictable and unstable
- Paradox and contradictions exist
- Need for ideas and innovation

COMPLICATED

- There are knowns and unknowns
- We can forecast or guess but it is hard to definitely know
- Experts are needed
- Situational analysis needed

CHAOTIC

- There are unknowables!
- High turbulence and tension
- No patterns seem to exist
- No time to think
- Many decisions to make . . . now

CLEAR

- The knowns are known
- Familiar and known patterns
- Wide agreement on cause and effect
- We have the facts and they are indisputable
- Obvious and agreed-on solutions

There are two specific things that you can do immediately to make context more real and useful in your organization.

First, people need to know what this "context stuff" is. Once people see where they are on the Context Map, they will have a better perspective. That's why providing training to team members on the simplified version of the Cynefin Framework is so important to your ultimate success. Any time people are trying to apply new skills, they will be far more successful if they are supported in practicing those skills by the people around them. Giving everyone a sense of the different contexts their situations might sit in will be empowering for the team and support the growth of the leader. This might cascade down or be provided to teams when their leader has begun their own journey toward Flexible Leadership.

Once people understand this context framework, they need to use it. That means using it in formal meetings and informal settings and thinking and talking about context when looking at problems, challenges, or opportunities as they arise. This creates organizational/team intentionality by consciously identifying the context of a situation up front. This supports the leader but also helps the team gain commitment and clarity on the process and next steps too.

Making context a part of your organizational language and culture will support your leaders' growth as Flexible Leaders, will help your team be more committed to both their work and changes they see in their leader, and hold everyone accountable to creating better and more sustainable results.

Culture

This isn't a book about team or organizational culture, but you can't integrate any organizational change (and creating more flexible leaders is one such change) without considering culture. We define culture as "the way we do things around here," which is like saying that culture is the collective habits of the group, team, or organization.

While I don't know the specifics of your culture, I do know that creating Flexible Leaders and expecting Flexible Leadership will, at the very least, adjust it in some ways. After all, if your leaders begin to lead differently, "the way we do things around here" will inevitably change.

You likely don't need a full-scale renovation of your culture, but you do need to think about appropriate adjustments to it. The simplest example is to add the idea of context to your everyday conversations.

We have helped many organizations and teams with intentional cultural change efforts, and we outline our approach in our book *The Long-Distance Team*.

Training and Learning

Since Flexible Leadership isn't intuitively obvious or easy, if you want more flexible leaders, you need to give them some training and education. But what that looks like will be different from one organization to another. Since consulting in a one-way conversation like a book is difficult, I'm moving into questioning mode . . .

If you have some existing in-house or externally delivered leadership training, start with this big question: *Can we integrate or augment our existing training to include these principles, or do we need to start over?*

Here are some questions to help you think about that:

- How does our existing training connect with the principles and practices of Flexible Leadership?
- Are there components we need to adjust, change, or remove?
- Do we need to rethink the amount of focus we place on a style assessment or how we teach it?

- Can we add Flexible Leadership principles to what we already have in place?
- Do we need to add a new learning experience to what we already have?
- Do we need or want to start over?

If you don't have any existing leadership training, or it is very limited, start with this question: *Do we have the internal resources needed to create the training and learning we need?*

Depending on your answer to that question, here are some additional questions to consider:

- How committed is senior leadership to investing time and money to develop our leaders?
- How can I/we build (or create) that commitment?
- Do we have existing leadership competencies or identified skills we can tie to this work?
- Do we have internal resources to design, develop, and deliver this training?
- If not, are we willing to add these resources or work with a partner?

Once you have decided to integrate or implement these mindsets, skillsets, and habitsets in your organization, remember that training alone won't be enough. The Flexible Leadership Approach requires us to think differently and, in most cases, change our habits. That means ongoing support, encouragement, and reinforcement is needed to create better results. That's why the more of these components you incorporate, the more effective you will be in changing how the leaders in your organization lead.

- *Set context for the journey.* Help leaders understand the value and importance of these new mindsets, skillsets, and habitsets at the start of their learning journey. And make sure they see it as a journey, not simply a training course. The better prepared people are mentally, the more open and ready they will be to learn new skills.

- *Make it meaningful.* Meaning will come from tying the new skills to the why of the work. Meaning is further strengthened when leaders see their leaders being accountable for learning and applying the same skills. This is key to your organizational leadership transformation.

- *Provide peer support.* Changing habits and existing patterns is hard to do. Having a peer as a specific learning partner to be a coach, encourager, and sounding board can be extremely valuable. These partnerships also offer one of the most powerful forms of accountability—which is helpful in changing any habit. In addition, being the partner helps us build our skills and confidence in the new skills while we are helping our colleague. Peer support can also include online forums, chat groups, or channels. The more ways people can learn from, assist, and support each other, the faster skills and confidence will grow.

- *Provide a multisensory ongoing learning experience.* Consider ways to extend the learning beyond an event. This might include text or email reminders, short videos, additional learning in different formats, and a mix of media. If you are working with a provider as a partner, tell them you want ongoing and blended learning.

- *Include coaching.* The best performers in any endeavor, including leadership, have coaches. The peer learning partner is one avenue for coaching but may not be the only one you want or need. Whether the coaching comes from internally trained coaches, external coaches, or as an enhanced role of the leader's leader, make coaching specifically tied to leading with greater flexibility part of your learning process.

Integration

The steps in this chapter are a specific description of one of our core beliefs: that *training is an event, but learning is a process.*

When you take the five steps we've just explored, you have set the table for the integration of Flexible Leadership principles and practices into your organization in deep and meaningful ways. Just "doing some training" or having a book club based on this book may help only some leaders improve. The individual improvement/change may not last without support and reinforcement.

Admittedly, it is more work to take a holistic approach as we have described here. It will likely be different than what you have implemented before. But like the Flexible Leadership Approach itself, it requires us to do some different things—outside of our habits and normal approaches.

If you want the strong, powerful ripples in the pond of your organization, where all leaders are transforming the organization by the way they lead, this overall approach will get you there. The more of these steps you leave out or try to rush, the less likely you will gain the advantages and benefits Flexible Leadership can bring to your organization.

PAUSE AND REFLECT

Before you move on, take a minute to think about these questions. (Even better if you take some notes on your thoughts!)

- Where are we on the road map?
- How can we attach these ideas to what we are already doing in developing our leaders?
- How will this change impact our organizational results?
- Who do I/we need to influence?
- What is our best next step?

RESOURCES TO HELP YOU LEAD FLEXIBLY

You can learn more about a process for identifying and intentionally moving toward your aspirational organizational culture in our book *The Long-Distance Team*.

If you want help thinking through or implementing your options for training and supporting your Flexible Leaders, you can reach out to us.

You can get more information about both at FlexibleLeadership-Book.com or by scanning this QR code.

Meaning will come from tying the new skills to the why of the work. Meaning is further strengthened when leaders see their leaders being accountable for learning and applying the same skills. This is key to your organizational leadership transformation.

CONCLUSION

The Message

Consider this as my overall message to you, my fellow leader. I hope you will read this and let the words sink in. I hope that this resonates with, encourages, and inspires you. I hope that you will return to this message often, rereading it to refill your emotional and spiritual cups.

———

The world needs leaders.

Because nothing positive happens in the world without someone leading.

The world needs you to lead.

Not because of your position or title, but because you have something unique that you can contribute.

But while you can be part of a magical solution to the world's problems, challenges, and maladies, potential isn't enough.

Make no mistake, you have that potential, but potential without action is a waste—the saddest story that can be told.

Consider the acorn. Is the acorn the seed for one tree, or for untold future trees? It can be all of that, but until it is planted, it can be none of it. There is great potential in the acorn, but it is wasted if it lies on concrete.

You are like an acorn—full of potential to make a difference in so many ways.

Remember the three Os of leadership: outcomes, others, and ourselves.

You can influence amazing and meaningful outcomes for your team, in your organization, and across the world.

You can touch, inspire, and change the lives of others for the better. As a leader, you can help people find meaning and show them their inner acorns too.

And leadership is about you too—who you are makes a difference in how you lead and the results you get. But staying the same without growing, developing, and changing is like placing yourself on the concrete next to the acorn.

You *can* accomplish and impact all of those things. But will you?

"Can" is the acorn on concrete.

Just because you can doesn't mean you will.

Will requires choice.

Will is planting yourself in fertile soil.

As a human, you have the power of choice. No other living thing has this powerful ability. The ability to look at your situation and choose what to do.

Here is one of the most profound pieces of advice you will ever hear. It comes from Og Mandino, a businessman and an author of many books. Og wrote this profound truth: *Use wisely your power of choice.*[38]

It is your choice to use your potential to change the world, your organization, your team, and yourself.

It is your choice to move beyond your natural and habitual responses and do something differently.

It is your choice to consider the context of the situation to determine the best course of action.

It is your choice to flex your responses and approaches to better match the needs of the outcomes and those doing the work.

These choices aren't easy. They are often counter to what you have been told about what leadership is and what you have told yourself about yourself.

But these are choices you can make.

And when you make them, they will make all the difference for you and your team.

Making these choices can be hard but can also sometimes be unpopular. The statesman Henry Kissinger once said, "A leader does not deserve the name unless he is willing occasionally to stand alone."[39]

As a leader, you do stand alone. You must point the way to places unseen. You must shoulder responsibilities others don't see. It isn't always easy.

But you can do it.

If you are thinking backward, questioning yourself, stop.

I know you have made mistakes.

Every person, and every leader, has.

Leaders like you acknowledge and learn from those mistakes, knowing that they can make you stronger in the future.

Why?

Because leaders like you are learners.

You will learn from your mistakes.

You will reflect on your successes and missteps—both big and small.

You will seek out wise sources of knowledge.

You will listen, think, and try new things.

You were born to be a Remarkable Flexible Leader. It is up to you to choose to use your experiences, background, and purpose to tap that potential.

To claim it.

To believe it.

Maybe what you most need to know is that someone believes in you.

I believe in you.

I know you have potential.

I know that when you truly see the positive impact you can have, you will plant your acorn.

I know you can lead in ways that can make a big difference—whether within your team, across your organization, or yes, even for the whole world.

When you choose.

Being a Flexible Leader starts with the choices.

The choices are yours.

And your choices can unlock a world of possibility, opportunity, and excitement.

I hope you see what I see.

Because if you do, you will move from "can" and "could" to "will" and "am."

From possibility and potential to remarkable results.

The world, your organization, and your team need you . . .

To become the leader you were born to be.

SUGGESTED READING

Bennis, Warren G., and Burt Nanus. *Leaders: Strategies for Taking Charge, Second Edition.* New York: Harper Business, 2007.

Berger, Warren. *The Book of Beautiful Questions: The Powerful Questions That Will Help You Decide, Create, Connect, and Lead.* New York: Bloomsbury Publishing, 2018.

Brougham, Greg. *The Cynefin Mini-Book: An Introduction to Complexity and the Cynefin Framework.* Morrisville, NC: Lulu.com, 2015.

Clear, James. *Atomic Habits: An Easy & Proven Way to Build Good Habits & Break Bad Ones.* New York: Avery, 2018.

Eikenberry, Kevin. *Remarkable Leadership: Unleashing Your Leadership Potential One Skill at a Time.* San Francisco: Jossey-Bass, 2007.

Eikenberry, Kevin. *Unleashing Your Remarkable Potential* newsletter. KevinEikenberry.com/newsletter.

Eikenberry, Kevin, and Guy Harris. *From Bud to Boss: Secrets to a Successful Transition to Remarkable Leadership.* San Francisco: Jossey-Bass, 2011

Eikenberry, Kevin, and Wayne Turmel. *The Long-Distance Leader: Revised Rules for Remarkable Remote and Hybrid Leadership.* Oakland: Berrett-Koehler Publishers, 2024.

Eikenberry, Kevin, and Wayne Turmel. *The Long-Distance Team: Designing Your Team for the Modern Workplace*. Washington, DC: National Geographic Books, 2023.

Epstein, David. *Range: Why Generalists Triumph in a Specialized World*. New York: Riverhead Books, 2019.

Gladwell, Malcolm. *Outliers: The Story of Success*. New York: Back Bay Books, 2011.

Goodall, Ashley. *The Problem with Change: And the Essential Nature of Human Performance*. New York: Little, Brown Spark, 2024.

Kahneman, Daniel. *Thinking, Fast and Slow*. New York: Farrar, Strauss and Giroux, 2011.

Madsbjerg, Christian. *Sensemaking: The Power of the Humanities in the Age of the Algorithm*. New York: Hatchette Books, 2017.

Northhouse, Peter. *Leadership: Theory and Practice, Ninth Edition*. Thousand Oaks, CA: SAGE Publications, 2021.

Smith, Wendy, and Marianne Lewis. *Both/And Thinking: Embracing Creative Tensions to Solve Your Toughest Problems*. Brighton, MA: Harvard Business Review Press, 2022.

Snowden, Dave, et al. *Cynefin—Weaving Sense-Making into the Fabric of Our World*, eds. Riva Greenberg, Boudesijn Bertsch. Colwyn Bay, Wales, UK: Cognitive Edge, the Cynefin Company, 2020.

Snowden, Dave, and Mary E. Boone. "A Leader's Framework for Decision Making." *Harvard Business Review*, November 2007, https://hbr.org/2007/11/a-leaders-framework-for-decision-making.

Steinberg, Pete. *Leadership Shock: Using Authenticity to Navigate the Hidden Dangers of Career Success*. Charleston, SC: Advantage Media Group, 2024.

Stulberg, Brad. *Master of Change: How to Excel When Everything Is Changing—Including You.* San Francisco: HarperOne, 2023.

ter Kuile, Casper. *The Power of Ritual: Turning Everyday Activities into Soulful Practices.* San Francisco: HarperOne, 2021.

Wooden, John, and Steve Jamison. *Wooden on Leadership: How to Create a Winning Organization.* New York: McGraw Hill, 2005.

ABOUT THE KEVIN EIKENBERRY GROUP

I hope this book has challenged and inspired you to become a more flexible leader. And I know that a book, while a valuable tool, is rarely all we need on our leadership journey.

The Kevin Eikenberry Group has been helping leaders become more effective, confident, and successful since 1993.

And we'd like to continue to help you.

We offer a variety of learning, coaching, and consulting services to help leaders and organizations succeed. Along with our expertise in developing Flexible Leaders, we have extensive experience in working with teams, new and frontline leaders, and leaders of leaders—including helping with specific challenges and opportunities if people work virtually some or all of the time.

I know this book is just the tip of the iceberg in your leadership journey. Here are just a few of the other ways we can work together.

More learning opportunities. We offer a variety of learning opportunities, from keynotes and live learning events and workshops—both in-person and virtually delivered—to trainer certification, to on-demand offerings, blended learning approaches, and e-learning tools that provide targeted and just-in-time learning.

More help. If you are looking for tailored learning options inside your organization, coaching for one or more leaders, or guidance with broader organizational needs, we can help.

More tools. We offer a variety of free online resources to help you and your organization succeed. Our blog shares lessons from clients and our latest thinking on leadership, organizational development, and the continually evolving picture of the remote working world. Explore our website for this resource and our collection of learning tools and resources.

- All resources from this book can be found at FlexibleLeadershipBook.com.
- Our products and services, blog, and much more can be found at KevinEikenberry.com.
- Sign up for our free newsletters at KevinEikenberry.com /newsletters.
- Sign up for our unique video series, *13 Days to Remarkable Leadership*, at KevinEikenberry.com/13Days.
- Contact us at info@KevinEikenberry.com if you want a free consultation about how we can help you transform your leaders into more flexible leaders.
- Connect with us on LinkedIn for regular content and to let me know how else we can assist you and your organization.

You can access a page with all of these links, as well as links to the resources provided throughout this book, at the QR code below.

 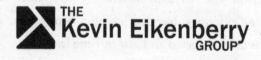

ACKNOWLEDGMENTS

Even if writing a book is a solitary activity, you never do it alone. There are many whose handprints and heart prints are a part of making this book a reality. Because I have been doing the work of leadership—studying it, teaching it, coaching it, and doing it myself—the number of people who have played a part in the ideas I have shared are literally innumerable.

There are some groups and individuals that need to be singled out and thanked.

The authors who have inspired and taught me. Many are mentioned on the pages of this book and in the suggested reading list. But there are more. As of this writing, I have interviewed more than 600 authors and experts for *The Remarkable Leadership Podcast*, Virtual LeaderCon, and other purposes. Each has given me insights and ideas. Without all of you, I would not have been able to craft what I hope is a coherent and valuable step forward in leadership thinking.

The team at BenBella Books, starting with Matt Holt. Matt believed in me before I even gave him this book idea. I hope it makes him proud to have his name on it. Lydia Choi, who helped me craft the words here with valuable insight, suggestions, and counsel. Morgan Carr is largely responsible for the cover of the book—I am grateful for your insight and skill. There are more on the team I haven't worked with yet, as of this writing, but their contributions will be equally important. I thank you all.

To the readers and other contributors. Thanks to Jim Huling for the gracious foreword, to the others whose kind words of endorsement are an honor, and to those who read the first draft of the book—all of whom helped make it better: Jodi Dubuclet, Guy Harris, Adrienne Knox, Rob Simmerman, and Josh Zimmet. I (and every reader) will be forever grateful to you.

To my team at the Kevin Eikenberry Group. I have learned from all of you, past and present. For those who were there during 2024, I thank you for your patience with me as I wrote the book, when you might have wanted a little more of my focus, time, and effort. I thank you in advance for all you will do to help promote and get this book into the world. A big thanks to Guy Harris and Wayne Turmel—two members of our team I have written books with in the past. Working with you has made me a better writer, which is hopefully reflected here. A special thank-you to Erica Brown, who created all the images in the book and took the photo on the jacket flap. Working with this subject matter alone (me!) should be proof of her talent.

To my family. To Alan, George, Jamie, and Tom—brothers from other mothers who are always there for me and remind and teach me so much about life, and, as a result, leadership. I am a better man because of these guys. To Parker and Kelsey, my children who taught me so much, and whom I failed too often, I hope you know how much I love you. To Marisa—who could have been mentioned in the last paragraph too—thanks for putting up with me as a boss and a father-in-law. To Haaris—I hope you are as happy to be joining this family as we are to have you. To my mom, whose wisdom and love is a part of me always, and to my dad, who I miss every day and hear sometimes as I write.

And to Lori, the love of my life who has taught me so much, loved me so hard, and put up with me for so long. I am not the writer, leader, or person I am without you.

Finally, to God—my creator. For His forgiveness, grace, and love, and for the promises for the future.

NOTES

1. Claudio Feser, Nicolai Nielsen, and Michael Rennie, "What's Missing in Leadership Development?" *McKinsey Quarterly*, August 1, 2017, https://www.mckinsey.com/featured-insights/leadership/whats-missing-in-leadership-development.
2. Aarushi Tewari, "60+ New Beginnings Quotes for a Fresh Start," *Gratitude* (blog), accessed August 30, 2024, https://blog.gratefulness.me/new-beginnings-quotes/.
3. Merriam-Webster.com Dictionary, s. v. "Flexible," accessed June 15, 2024, https://www.merriam-webster.com/dictionary/flexible.
4. Ashley Goodall, *The Problem with Change: And the Essential Nature of Human Performance* (New York: Little, Brown Spark, 2024).
5. Christian Madsbjerg, *Sensemaking: The Power of the Humanities in the Age of the Algorithm* (New York: Hachette Books, 2017).
6. K. Weick, K. M. Sutcliffe, and D. Obstfeld, "Organizing and the Process of Sensemaking," *Organization Science* 16, no. 4 (2005): 409–21, doi: 10.1287/orsc.1050.0133.
7. Deborah Ancona, "Sensemaking: Framing and Acting in the Unknown," in *The Handbook for Teaching Leadership: Knowing, Doing, and Being*, eds. Scott Snook, Nitin Nohria, and Rakesh Khurana (Thousand Oaks, CA: SAGE Publications, 2012): 3–20.
8. David J. Snowden and Mary E. Boone, "A Leader's Framework for Decision Making," *Harvard Business Review*, November 2007, https://hbr.org/2007/11/a-leaders-framework-for-decision-making.

9. Dave Snowden et al, *Cynefin—Weaving Sense-Making into the Fabric of Our World*, eds. Riva Greenberg and Boudesijn Bertsch (Colwyn Bay, Wales, UK: Cognitive Edge, the Cynefin Company, 2020).

10. Transcript of Defense Department Briefing, February 12, 2002, accessed August 30, 2024, https://usinfo.org/wf-archive/2002/020212/epf202.htm.

11. David S. Pugh, *Organization Theory: Selected Readings: Fourth Edition* (London: Penguin UK, 1997).

12. Brad Stulberg, *Master of Change: How to Excel When Everything Is Changing—Including You* (San Francisco: HarperOne, 2023).

13. Peter Sterling and Joseph Eyer, "Allostasis: A New Paradigm to Explain Arousal Pathology," in *Handbook of Life Stress, Cognition and Health*, eds. Shirley Fisher and James Reason (Hoboken, NJ: John Wiley & Sons, 1988), 629–49.

14. F. Scott Fitzgerald, "The Crack-Up," *Esquire*, February 1, 1936, https://classic.esquire.com/article/share/97a6b0a8-ba1c-4b7b-aa64-0d08dd9fb952.

15. Wendy Smith and Marianne Lewis, *Both/And Thinking: Embracing Creative Tensions to Solve Your Toughest Problems* (Brighton, MA: Harvard Business Review Press, 2022).

16. Daniel Kahneman, *Thinking, Fast and Slow* (New York: Farrar, Straus and Giroux, 2011).

17. Wayne W. Dyer, *The Power of Intention: Learning to Co-create Your World Your Way* (Carlsbad, CA: Hay House, 2004).

18. Ani DiFranco, *Verses* (New York: Seven Stories Press, 2007).

19. Greg Brougham, *The Cynefin Mini-Book: An Introduction to Complexity and the Cynefin Framework* (Morrisville, NC: Lulu.com, 2015).

20. Okakura Kakuzo, *The Book of Tea* (New York: Macmillan Collector's Library, 2020).

21. Oren Harari, "Quotations from Chairman Powell: A Leadership Primer," GovLeaders.org, accessed August 30, 2024, https://govleaders.org/powell.htm.

22. Thomas J. Peters and Robert H. Waterman Jr., *In Search of Excellence: Lessons from America's Best-Run Companies* (New York: Harper Business, 2006).

23. "Core Values & Heritage," Marriott International website, accessed August 30, 2024, https://www.marriott.com/culture-and-values/core -values.mi.

24. John Wooden and Steve Jamison, *Wooden on Leadership: How to Create a Winning Organization* (New York: McGraw Hill, 2005).

25. Malcolm Gladwell, *Outliers: The Story of Success* (New York: Back Bay Books, 2011).

26. David Epstein, *Range: Why Generalists Triumph in a Specialized World* (New York: Riverhead Books, 2019).

27. Goodhart's law is often generalized with this quote, which originally comes from anthropologist Marilyn Strathern: Marilyn Strathern, "'Improving Ratings': Audit in the British University System," *European Review* 5, no. 3 (July 1997): 305–321, doi: 10.1002/(SICI)1234 -981X(199707)5:3<305::AID-EURO184>3.0.CO;2-4.

28. Will Durant, *The Story of Philosophy: The Lives and Opinions of the Greater Philosophers* (Berkeley, CA: Mint Editions, 2024 [originally published 1926]).

29. Stan Slap, *Bury My Heart at Conference Room B: The Unbeatable Impact of Truly Committed Managers* (New York: Portfolio, 2010).

30. Peter Northouse, *Leadership: Theory and Practice, Ninth Edition* (Thousand Oaks, CA: SAGE Publications, 2021).

31. Warren Bennis and Burt Nanus, *Leaders: Strategies for Taking Charge, Second Edition* (New York: Harper Business, 2007).

32. Bohdi Sanders, *Men of the Code: Living as a Superior Man* (Loveland, CO: Kaizen Quest, 2015).

33. Robert Collier, *Riches Within Your Reach!* (New York: TarcherPerigee, reissue edition, 2009).

34. James Clear, *Atomic Habits: An Easy & Proven Way to Build Good Habits & Break Bad Ones* (New York: Avery, 2018).

35. Ryder Carroll, "Habit vs. Ritual," Medium, May 29, 2021, https://rydercarroll.medium.com/habit-vs-ritual-2c8cbca6e4ad.

36. Casper ter Kuile, *The Power of Ritual: Turning Everyday Activities into Soulful Practices* (San Francisco: HarperOne, 2021).

37. "Remarks Prepared for Delivery at the Trade Mart in Dallas, TX, November 22, 1963 [Undelivered]," John F. Kennedy Presidential Library and Museum, accessed August 30, 2024, https://www.jfklibrary.org/archives/other-resources/john-f-kennedy-speeches/dallas-tx-trade-mart-undelivered-19631122.

38. Og Mandino, *The Greatest Miracle in the World* (New York: Bantam, reissue edition, 1983).

39. Henry Kissinger, *The Necessity for Choice: Prospects of American Foreign Policy, First Edition* (New York: HarperCollins, 1961).

ABOUT THE AUTHOR

Photo by Erica Brown

Kevin is the Chief Potential Officer of the Kevin Eikenberry Group, a leadership and learning consulting company that has been helping organizations, teams, and individuals reach their potential since 1993.

The team's clients include leaders from over 50 countries, Fortune 500 companies, small firms, universities, government agencies, hospitals, and more. Inc.com has twice named him in the top 100 Leadership and Management Experts in the World, and Global Gurus has listed him in the top 30 Leadership Professionals in the World for three years running. He is the author, coauthor, or contributing author of nearly 20 books that have been published in at least seven languages.

He is the developer of a variety of innovative leadership development programs including Virtual LeaderCon and was the cofounder of the Remote Leadership Institute.

His e-learning programs are available on most of the major platforms, including LinkedIn Learning, where his courses have been translated into 13 languages.

Kevin writes several email newsletters, and his writing has been featured in newspapers, magazines, trade journals, and websites from around the world, including a monthly column for BusinessManagementDaily.com. He hosts *The Remarkable Leadership Podcast* with over 800 episodes, and RemarkableTV, a YouTube channel with over 540 weekly episodes.

Kevin lives with his wife, Lori, in Indianapolis, Indiana. He is a proud graduate of the Purdue College of Agriculture, collects antique John Deere tractors, is an avid reader, enjoys smoking meat and cheese, and loves God, his family, his team at the Kevin Eikenberry Group, and his Boilermakers.